3 0214 1010 2473 6   Sams   4/13/06   25.99

D0959842

DISCARD

ARUBA

ARUBA

*The Tragic Untold Story of Natalee Holloway
and Corruption in Paradise*

Dave Holloway

with

R. Stephanie Good

and

Larry Garrison

NELSON CURRENT

A Subsidiary of Thomas Nelson, Inc.

Published in Nashville, Tennessee, by Nelson Current, a division of a wholly owned subsidiary (Nelson Communications, Inc.) of Thomas Nelson, Inc.

Nelson Current books may be purchased in bulk for educational, business, fundraising, or sales promotional use. For information, please e-mail SpecialMarkets@ThomasNelson.com.

**Library of Congress Cataloging-in-Publication Data
on file with the Library of Congress.**

Holloway, Dave.
    Aruba : the tragic untold story of Natalee Holloway and corruption in paradise / Dave Holloway with R. Stephanie Good and Larry Garrison.
        p. cm.
    ISBN 1-59555-063-1
    1. Holloway, Natalee. 2. Missing children—Aruba. 3. Missing persons—Aruba. 4. Young women—Crimes against—Aruba. I. Good, R. Stephanie. II. Garrison, Larry. III. Title.
HV6762.A75H65 2006
362.8—dc22   2006002714

Printed in the United States of America

06 07 08 09 10 QW 5 4 3 2 1

I dedicate this book to my daughter
Natalee,
for your love, your beautiful smile, and your inspiration,
and for teaching me that giving up is never an option.

Contents

Acknowledgments

THERE ARE LITERALLY THOUSANDS OF PEOPLE WHO have helped us during our ordeal, physically, emotionally, monetarily, or through their prayers.

I want to start by thanking my wonderful wife, Robin, who has provided endless support and love.

My children Matt, Brooke, and Kaitlyn who fill my heart with peace and joy and make each new day a little brighter than the last.

My mother, Chris Holloway; my brothers, Steve Holloway, Phil Holloway, and Todd Vestal; my sister, Linda Allison; my mother-in-law and father-in-law, Carol and Melvin Parten; my brothers-in-law, Michael and Steve Parten, who have all joined in our search, held us up when we needed support, and kept our heartache from completely overwhelming us.

My father, Jack Holloway, who has watched over us and given us strength during these difficult months.

My church and community for surrounding us with their warmth and comfort.

My State Farm colleagues and policyholders, the many total strangers who sent their good wishes, and the many strangers who became our friends.

The search teams, especially Tim Miller and Equusearch, Art

Wood, and Patrick Murphy; the Internet bloggers; the news media; the politicians; and some of the good people of Aruba who truly care about seeking answers and justice for Natalee.

The persons who have made this book possible:

Larry Garrison, for knowing how to open the right doors for opportunities and for your brilliance in making things happen.

Stephanie Good, for your creativity, knowledge, and the ability to write a *New York Times* bestseller.

And finally, the teams at Nelson Current and Waterside Productions for making this book a reality.

God bless you all!

ONE

Everybody's Child

I CANNOT TELL YOU HOW MUCH IT HURTS TO LOSE A child. There are no words to describe the feelings that choke a parent who outlives a daughter. It is not supposed to happen this way. I was never prepared for this kind of pain, this type of emptiness. My heart has an insurmountable void that used to be filled with Natalee's presence.

I watched as she received her high school diploma, and I took pictures of her at her graduation ceremony. I planned to be there when she graduated from college and then medical school. My pride would have enveloped us both. I had long imagined the day when I would see my Natalee in her beautiful white wedding gown. We would meet in the back of the church for her last moment as "daddy's little girl" and, as she encircled my arm with hers, I would lean down and whisper the words that all fathers must say to their daughters on that very special day, "I love you." I would walk her down the aisle and proudly offer her hand to her fiancé, and I would return to my seat knowing that my girl had accomplished all that a father could desire. At that moment, it would be clear that the first tier of her life with me had come to an end and that the man she would now look to for approval and love would be her husband. But she would always be my little Natalee . . . always.

When Natalee and her brother Matt were young, we lived in Clinton, Mississippi. We had been building some very special memories, but lately it has been difficult to recall them without a lot of pain. I try to picture Natalee riding her bike around the neighborhood, or envision the excited expression on her face when she woke up on Christmas morning and spotted the toys we had stayed up half the night putting together. I remember how she loved climbing up onto my back as I crawled along the floor on my hands and knees and how when she wanted to show off her dancing, she jumped up on her miniature table to do a routine and it tipped over, throwing her off and breaking her arm. I think back to her first days of kindergarten when she was only five and how I drove her up to school every morning and walked her to class to show her around and get her used to it. I can still see her sad little face during the second week when I told her it was time to go in on her own. She still wanted Daddy to walk her to class. I keep thinking back because I'm so afraid that if I don't, the memories will begin to fade. And, for now, that is all I have of her to hold on to.

Natalee was seven and Matt was five when their mother, Beth, and I divorced in 1993. After I remarried in 1995, my wife, Robin, and I lived in Jackson, Mississippi, but we relocated back to Clinton in 1996 to be close to Natalee and Matt. When Beth remarried in 2000, she and her husband, Jug, moved to Mountain Brook, Alabama, and Robin and I moved to Meridian, Mississippi, where our two daughters, Brooke and Kaitlyn, were born. Natalee and Matt live in Mountain Brook with Beth and Jug and visit us in Mississippi as often as their schedules allow. Prior to Natalee's sixteenth birthday and obtaining her driver's license, she and Matt had been coming to our home every other weekend and more frequently during their summer vacations from school. But, during Natalee's senior year in high school, her visits were a bit less frequent due to her many extracurricular activities. So Robin and I made it our business to visit her and watch her dance at football games with her dance team, the Dorians.

Robin and I have maintained a close, loving relationship with Natalee throughout her childhood and teenage years. We have tried to instill certain values and traits in all of our children that would enable them to succeed in life. Those values include honesty, integrity, morality, and a deep faith in God. We believe that Natalee has a solid foundation in those values. Robin and I have our own set of faith-based values that guide us in our daily lives. At this time of upheaval, we have gained strength from our reliance upon those values. We have felt God's presence every step of the way, and that is what has sustained us in these, our darkest hours of need.

Natalee is missing.

I desperately want her back.

From the moment that she was born on October 21, 1986, she has always been an exceptional human being. A father could not ask for more from a child. Her younger sisters lovingly call her Sissy, and she is a sensitive, loving, and articulate young woman. She is blessed with being beautiful both inside and out.

As Natalee completed her senior year, we were all excited about her next stepping stone in life. She was prepared to go off to the University of Alabama on a full scholarship to major in premed after graduating with honors and a 4.15 grade point average from Mountain Brook High School. She participated in numerous extracurricular activities, including the dance team and the Bible Club, and she was a member of both the math and Spanish honor societies. She had a part-time job at a health food store and performed volunteer work. She has some great friends, is well-traveled, and has always looked toward the future. She never showed any interest in drugs or alcohol, and she kept close ties with her siblings and classmates who all care for her very much.

In February 2005, Natalee called me and asked for permission to go on a trip to Aruba with her graduating class. This is apparently a rite of passage for teenagers all over the country. They convince their parents to allow this one-time privilege as a gift for all of their hard work, and parents often agree, even when their instincts tell them otherwise. I was apprehensive about Natalee taking this type of trip, and I tried to talk her out of it. I did not like the idea of her traveling that far away with so many other students and so few chaperones.

When I received the trip brochure I saw that the cost was approximately $985. Robin and I are from the old school, and we felt that was a bit extravagant for a high school graduation trip. After a few days of consideration, I told Natalee that we could not approve of the trip for two reasons: it was too extravagant, and we did not think it was appropriate. However, I told her that I would give her a graduation gift of half the amount of the cost of the trip for her to do with as she pleased. Since Natalee's stepbrother had been to Aruba with his class two years earlier, and her twin cousins were graduating with her class and were going along with her this year, Beth felt comfortable allowing Natalee to make the trip.

The months passed, and upon receiving the invitation to Natalee's graduation, she advised us that the school had opted to hold the ceremony at a local university theater hall. Due to the limited amount of seating, each graduate was allocated only eight tickets. We were to have three of them for my wife, Robin, Natalee's grandmother, and me. That left her two sisters out. Due to the distance, I asked Natalee if she could get two more tickets for her sisters otherwise Robin might have had to stay behind to care for them. As graduation weekend drew near, Natalee and I spoke again of the tickets, and she assured me that she would call all three hundred of her classmates if she had to in order to come up with them. On Monday, May 23, we heard from Natalee, and, in a hoarse voice, she told us that after calling nearly every student, she was finally able to get us the tickets. She said that she was just not going to give up on us. I praised her determination.

On graduation day, we arrived at Natalee's home expecting to rush up to the door, grab the tickets, and leave. Instead, she insisted that her two sisters come in to see her room. Natalee's grandparents, Beth's mother and mine, also wanted to catch up, so Robin and I and the family spent about forty-five minutes in my ex-wife's home. The situation was very unusual for us and somewhat awkward for me, but it was Natalee's big day. Looking back, I think that God had a hand in putting us all together on that very special day, the last day that we may be sharing a momentous occasion with Natalee.

As we were about to leave, Natalee informed us that she and her friends would be going somewhere after the graduation ceremonies, so she might not see us later on.

There were approximately three thousand people in attendance at graduation. When the ceremony ended, I realized that I hadn't given Natalee the gift we had brought, so we tried to locate her. Everyone had headed outside to a reception, but there were so many people, all wearing the same graduation gown, I just assumed that we would not see her again that day. I thought she might have already hooked up with her friends and left. We headed for the car, but Robin insisted that we go back to try to find her. Suddenly Natalee called my cell phone and said she wanted to see us. We communicated back and forth until we were able to locate each other. I gave her our graduation present, a check for $500. She was thrilled and thanked us. We hugged, and I took some photos. I mentioned the trip to Aruba and asked her to be careful. We all said our good-byes and left. Later that evening, she called to thank us again.

The day before Natalee was to leave for Aruba, she called and spoke to Robin. She told her how excited she was about the trip, and Robin once again strongly cautioned her to be careful. The next day, Natalee left with approximately 125 students and 7 chaperones. We heard that, upon their arrival in Aruba, the chaperones scheduled daily meetings with the students and collected their passports before distributing their room keys. Every day the students were to check in with the chaperones at a specific time.

On Monday, May 30, Natalee's trip came to an end, and she was due to fly home to Alabama. But late in the afternoon, I received a call from Matt telling me that Natalee had missed her flight and that Beth was getting on a plane to Aruba. She had told him to call me, but had no details yet. I attempted to get in touch with Beth. No answer. I googled hotels in Aruba and found a number for the Holiday Inn where the kids had been staying. I called and was able to talk to one of the trip chaperones who had stayed behind in Natalee's room. He filled me in about Natalee missing her flight. At the time, there was not much to go on. Someone from the U.S. Drug Enforcement Agency was there on vacation, and he made a few calls to the police. Apparently, they have the same rule that we have in the United States about waiting twenty-four hours before taking a report on a missing person. I would later find out that it is one of the very few rules or laws that the United States and Aruba have in common.

Beth had flown out of Birmingham on a friend's private jet as soon as she learned that Natalee had missed her flight. I contacted a commercial airline and booked the next flight out for 5:30 a.m. the following morning. I immediately started a checklist and packed my bags. I stayed in contact with Matt, and by around 10:00 p.m., some of the Mountain Brook kids who had arrived back in Birmingham indicated to him that Natalee left a bar with a nice kid who played soccer and was visiting Aruba from Holland. Some of the Mountain Brook boys said they sat with him around the poker table in a casino on the previous evening.

Later that night, Matt called again to tell me that Natalee's flight had been rebooked, and she would be coming home the next day. Someone from Delta Airlines had confirmed that a female had called and changed the flight. Matt felt that Natalee had simply missed her plane and rebooked it. I cancelled my flight, but I was still concerned because no one had heard from Natalee. The next morning, I started making more calls. I could not reach Beth, and I was unable to get a member of the Aruban police force to talk to me on the phone about Natalee. I called the Holiday Inn again, but nobody answered the phone in Natalee's room. By noon I learned that Natalee was not getting on the plane. I found out that it had been a chaperone from Natalee's group who had changed her flight in the hopes that she would reappear. It was then that I knew something tragic must have happened. I feared the worst, but prayed for a miracle. I hung up the phone and broke down. My mind was racing with so many "what ifs." Once I was able to regain my composure, I called my brothers, Phil, Steve, and Todd, and my brother-in-law, Michael. Phil, Michael, and I all tried to book flights out right away but could not get any until the next day. I tried to discourage my youngest brother, Todd, from coming. He was in bankruptcy and couldn't afford the trip. But he said he had to come, and he stayed behind to sell two of his vehicles just to get the money for the plane ticket. Steve, a fireman, had to make arrangements to get coverage for his job, so he also came in a little later on.

My pastor heard the news and called from out of town to pray with me over the phone. I can still hear his comforting words, "God, please give Dave and his family the strength to get through this." Our family is very strong, and we were determined to find out what happened to Natalee and bring her home.

My world was turned upside-down, and my emotions ran wild. I could barely function. I had to keep myself together in order to help Natalee. She needed me to find her. The search-and-rescue planning began immediately.

We left Meridian, Mississippi, on the evening of May 31, 2005. The flight to Aruba was long, and I was in a panic. On one hand, I was traveling there to bring Natalee home. On the other hand, I was afraid of the worst.

When I arrived in Aruba with my family, we hit the island running. We rented a car and immediately headed out to find a police station. There were only four on the island and I was amazed to find that the first two we entered knew nothing about Natalee's disappearance. We were then directed to a third one, the Noord Police Station. I walked in and said, "I'm Dave Holloway, and I need to talk to you about my daughter who is missing." A man in the back stood up and said, "How much money do you have?" That was how I first met Detective Dennis Jacobs, the investigator who was assigned to handle Natalee's case after Beth made a report to him upon her arrival on the island. I thought his comment about money was odd, but I ignored it and just tried to talk to him about finding Natalee.

Jacobs painted a scenario that questioned all of the beliefs and values that we had instilled in Natalee. He insinuated that she had met someone and fallen in love. "This happens all the time. She will probably show up in a few days," he theorized. "She was just partying hard," he added. "Don't worry. Just go down to Carlos'n Charlie's and have a beer." It was June 1, 2005, our first evening in Aruba, my daughter was missing and a detective was telling us to go to a local bar and have a beer. I couldn't believe what I was hearing. He said it was the hot spot for vacationing kids. "Maybe she will show up." In fact, he was so confident that she was just partying it up or on drugs that he told us this particular bar would be the best place to find her. However, he did warn us to watch our drinks very carefully, adding that sometimes people put drugs into them. When I talked about searching for Natalee, he questioned why we would want to do that.

He told us to go to Carlos'n Charlie's rather than the crack houses where he said that Beth's husband, Jug, and his friends had gone the night before. They went there due to information received from the police that a lot of the kids do drugs and party and that Natalee was probably with them. Jacobs told us that he had received reports that Jug's people were busting up the drug houses—he didn't want us going there and stirring things up too. He said we should leave any searching to the police, and if we had reason to believe that Natalee was in a crack house, we should call him and he would check it out. He then told us that the government controlled the crack houses in order to keep the drug addicts off the streets and away from where tourists shop and dine.

Jacobs also told us that the day before we arrived, he had interviewed the boys who eventually became the three main suspects in Natalee's disappearance, Joran van der Sloot, Deepak Kalpoe, and his brother Satish. Beth had informed him of them after receiving information about videotapes taken from the security cameras outside of the Holiday Inn and in the hotel's casino. It had been determined that they were the last people to be seen with her. Jacobs considered the boys' statements to be consistent in that they had all said that they dropped Natalee off at the hotel. However, I did not realize at the time that Beth had already told him that the tapes did not show Natalee returning to the Holiday Inn that night.

We left the police station in a state of shock. We couldn't believe the attitude of the detective. Just the fact that he asked how much money I had took me by surprise. What kind of question is that to ask the father of a missing child? It seemed as if he was not at all concerned about our daughter. But, since he was in charge of the investigation, we followed his instructions and traveled to Carlos'n Charlie's hoping to find out what had happened to Natalee. We arrived there at about 10:30 p.m. and what I found was not like anything I had envisioned. While customers must pass by a bouncer at the door, there was no indication that he was stopping anyone from entering. The bar was packed with teenagers doing Jell-O shots and sleazy-looking island boys preying on the beautiful young female tourists. The place has more than one bar, and people were dancing and singing in every corner of the bi-level establishment. It was an unbelievable scene, one that I wish I had known about before Natalee left on her trip. I did not want to stay inside, so we hung out around the street corners. In less than two hours, we probably experienced at least ten to fifteen offers from various drug dealers who wanted us to buy from them. *Some government control,* I thought. Out of curiosity, my brother asked one of them what he had. "Whatever you need," he answered. "I have it or I can get it." We managed to strike up conversations with some of them who confided that the "higher ups" wanted them to always remember one thing: while peddling their drugs, they were never to commit a crime against a tourist, especially any American around the cruise dock areas. Later that evening, we went back to the hotel and planned our next strategy.

The following day, we began searching the beaches and mountain areas in the morning; in the evening, we returned to the street corners looking for leads about Natalee. After several nights there, we were confronted by some of the stray drug addicts who had come into the tourist area with tips about Natalee. Apparently, Jug's friends had started handing out money for information about Natalee's whereabouts. We had heard that Beth and the people who were searching with her were handing out hundred dollar bills. Due to the information that we were receiving about drug use on the island, Beth's side of the family was pursuing the possibility of a drug-related kidnapping, and they were going into drug houses and driving around town.

One particular drug addict gave us a tip that Natalee was in a specific drug house operated by "Tanya and Jim." He said there was an escape door in the back of the house, and if we entered, she might be whisked away into a secret room. My brother Phil knew this was just a hoax as we had several others trying to get money from us for the same type of tip. The drug addicts were only interested in getting more money, and when word got out among them that the family was paying for tips, all of them wanted in on the action. Some asked us for $10, and when my brother began asking more questions without paying, the price dropped to $5. Phil started to walk off, and one man kept following him. He wanted money, any amount, and he finally yelled out, "Isn't she worth at least two bucks?" Phil was just about ready to bust him with a right-hand fist when an off-duty police officer walked by. The drug addict knew him by name and asked if he was on duty. He said no and kept walking. The drug addict then turned and walked off.

Meanwhile, I did some investigating and found out more about the locals Natalee met who had been hanging out with the students from her hometown. Apparently, the boys had been throwing around lies about where they were staying. We heard that one of them, Joran van der Sloot, the son of a Dutch justice official, did not reveal that he lived on the island, but instead led the girls to believe that he was a vacationing student from Holland staying at the Holiday Inn. He was the boy Matt had told me about and one of the three that Dennis Jacobs had questioned.

From what we had learned, on what was to be her last night in Aruba, witnesses saw Natalee leave Carlos'n Charlie's with the three locals, Joran van der Sloot, the Dutch boy, and Surinamese-born brothers Deepak and Satish Kalpoe. After that, she disappeared. When the boys were initially brought in for questioning, they all admitted having been with Natalee on the night of her disappearance, saying that they were at the bar but left there with her around 1:30 a.m. to take a fifteen-minute drive out to the lighthouse because she wanted to see it. They claimed to have brought her right back to the Holiday Inn where she was staying, and to have left her there with security guards who helped her inside because she was supposedly very intoxicated.

According to what we found out from the Mountain Brook students, Natalee had met Joran van der Sloot in a casino the day before she disappeared. It's inconceivable that Natalee would have gone off with any of those boys so late at night and voluntarily. Everything about their story was unsettling. I know my Natalee. She must have been forced or drugged to go with them, if she really did. And, if she did go with them, then the last men to see her alive were walking around free. That gave them more than enough time to get rid of any evidence that Natalee might have left behind with them.

Incredibly, the police did not feel there was a need to search for Natalee. My daughter was missing without a trace, and the police considered the situation a kid's prank, something that responsible children just go off and do on a whim. No way. I disagreed with their theory of what happened. I know my daughter. She would never worry her family like that, and there was no way that she would get involved with three strangers unless she did not know what she was doing.

There I was in Aruba, a strange place, searching for my little girl, not knowing where she was, how she was, or what had happened to her. As I reflected on what the police had told me, I realized that they were trying to use the most innocent details to create a motive for Natalee to have voluntarily disappeared. For instance, they had somehow seen the quote that she had put in her high-school yearbook. It was from Lynyrd Skynyrd's song "Freebird":

> If I leave here tomorrow
> Would you still remember me?
> For I must be traveling on now,
> 'Cause there's too many places I've got to see.

They wanted us to believe that those words were an indication that our daughter had been planning to leave of her own free will and that she needed to get away. Natalee had disappeared, leaving every one of her possessions, including her passport, behind in a hotel room. Their hypothesis simply does not make sense. She is not the type of person to be so irresponsible as to deliberately miss a plane flight home without a word. Not my Natalee!

From my first day on the island, I realized that I could not rely on the police to find my daughter. If they refused to search, we would organize and do it ourselves. We were able to obtain enough information to learn the route the boys had taken with Natalee. We decided to start the search at the California Lighthouse on the northwestern tip of the island and work our way back to the Holiday Inn. I enlisted about fifty tourists to help. We searched the ground area but did not do any type of digging at that time. Incredibly, a publicity agent named Carla, from a New York City firm that handles publicity for tourism in Aruba, tried to stop us from searching near the California Lighthouse, a tourist attraction, saying that it would be harmful to the island and bring too much negative media attention. She said she had even discussed it with Beth and that she had agreed. But I advised her that the search would go forward, no matter what kind of attention it brought. Natalee made a statement when giving us those graduation tickets: "I wasn't going to give up on you." And my statement to her now was, "I'm not going to give up on you either!"

While I was frustrated by the complete lack of police involvement, the process of an investigation wasn't completely foreign to me. My employment background includes sixteen years of investigation into auto accidents. Some of the cases I have dealt with involved lawsuits, and as a manager I had the opportunity to work closely with many attorneys. In fact, I managed a claim unit that supervised the litigation process prior to becoming an agent. During those years, I learned that in order to do a thorough investigation, whether in a criminal or civil case, a top priority while gathering evidence is patience. However, I also know that the first few days are always the most critical because, as time goes by, the evidence is increasingly difficult to obtain or is lost. Witnesses forget details or confuse them; important facts may be overlooked that could end up making or breaking the case. If the police were going to let those crucial days pass by without searching, then I was thankful that I was able to use my years of experience and knowledge in the investigation to do my own search for our daughter Natalee.

While Beth's side was taking care of most of the public areas, such as visiting schools, putting out posters in shops and public places, and riding around in vehicles at night chasing leads, my team focused on the ground search. The terrain on Aruba is unforgiving. The island is volcanic, and most of the land is uneven, jagged, pitted, rock formations. In some areas, if you fall without protection, you will cut yourself to shreds on the rocks. Almost all of the vegetation involves some sort of thorns, stickers, or cacti, including the trees and bushes. Due to the heat and rough terrain, it was similar to being in the desert. We searched through caves and other treacherous areas, and we came in every evening, sweaty, sunburned, cut up by thorns, briars, and most anything else we touched. It was an ordeal, but if we could find Natalee, it did not matter what we had to endure.

One day, while searching in a rocky area on the south side of the island, we surprised some mountain goats that were lazily sleeping in their safe cave hideout in a secluded inland mountain rock ridge overhang. I was probably the first human being that a couple of those baby goats had ever seen. Their parents trotted off out of the opposite end of the open cave while the young ones curiously watched as I sat on a rock and allowed myself to briefly let go. Tears ran down my face. I was worn out, and I was having one of those moments that I suppose was perfectly normal, under the circumstances. I still could not believe what was happening. How was it possible that I was in a foreign country searching for my missing daughter?

After a few minutes of much-needed rest, I regrouped, and we continued to clear the area. When we felt that we had exhausted our search there, we moved down to the beach and discussed our next plan of action. We searched by foot one day, by four-wheeler the next, and alternated with a four-wheel drive and walkers. We worked in groups of two each, for a total of four people, my brother, brother-in-law, and me. The other person was Patrick Murphy. He was from the Cayman Islands, and when he first saw Natalee's story break, he decided he would come to Aruba to help out. He joined in and assisted us for about two weeks. He said he was a little surprised when he found out that the three of us were conducting the search. The way we worked it was that two people would be let out of the vehicle. The second two would drive the vehicle approximately half a mile down the road at the southeast beach. They would get out and move forward. The other two would work toward the vehicle, then get in and drive past the other two and park the vehicle and continue to move forward. We each had radios to communicate.

During our daylight searches throughout the island, our group came across many abandoned houses where drug addicts had left razors and other drug paraphernalia. Some were filled with foul smelling odors, feces, urine, cardboard boxes they used as blankets or beds, and general trash. One of those houses was located right next to a fine restaurant near the hotel area and a McDonald's.

In a conversation with some locals, I was told that the island was a major shipment area and that drugs were abundant. After what I saw, I couldn't disagree. Several times, people came into the hotel to meet with other locals and an apparent drug deal was taking place. The person would come in to scope out the area prior to doing the deal. I witnessed a number of twenty-to-thirty-year-old couples entering the hotel after a hard night of partying, and it was obvious that their intoxicated state was from something other than alcohol. Where else could you go and have a weekend of crack or cocaine and return home without having to worry about being arrested for buying or using drugs? You certainly couldn't risk doing it that freely in the United States!

The days passed with no real leads and nothing to indicate whether Natalee was still alive. Hundreds of calls came in with tips that led nowhere and suggestions of crazy schemes that would try anyone's patience. We kept searching and praying. It was all we could do for Natalee, and we hoped it would be enough.

Aruba, being a Dutch protectorate, falls within the jurisdiction of the Dutch government, so I was told to arrive at the Coast Guard headquarters at 7:00 a.m. on Sunday, June 5, 2005, to meet with the captain of the Dutch Marines, along with some people from the police department. When everyone had assembled, I asked them what the plan was. They stared blankly at me and said that they were just told to show up and I would be in charge. I couldn't believe that I was expected to run the show, as though I knew their island better than they did, and well enough to tell them where to start looking. What an unbelievable situation! I wondered if they were either too incompetent to conduct a search on their own or whether they were trying to cover up a crime and hoping to appease me with the offer to look for Natalee wherever I suggested. Either way, it was incredibly frustrating, and it made me feel somewhat helpless. But I had brought a huge map with me that my team had been following and had crossed out where we had already searched. I showed them all where I thought they should begin. My brother and I arranged for the Dutch Marines to help search at the south end of the island in the sand dunes while we were going to search the area just south of the Holiday Inn in four-wheelers. We all agreed to meet back at the Holiday Inn at 11:00 a.m. to discuss our next move, then we left for our assigned areas. Phil rode in a police helicopter while Patrick and I split up and searched the beach.

Everything came to a sudden halt when the Dutch Marines found a bloody mattress in a shack on the beach. The media immediately swarmed the area. I went back to my hotel to notify everyone of the find. Thankfully, the blood turned out to be from a dog.

Not even a full week had passed, and I had become so engrossed in my daughter's disappearance that I was hardly aware of what was going on in the rest of the world. I had absolutely no idea that Natalee's situation had sparked widespread news coverage until I phoned home and heard about it from Robin. The only news channel that we were able to view in the hotel by the time we got back to our room late at night was CNN, and to hear from Robin that Natalee's picture was being broadcast all over the world was unbelievable. And it brought home the message that everyone, not just her family, took her situation seriously. I was glad to see that our plight had gained so much support in such a short time.

Natalee had become everybody's child.

TWO

No Body, No Case

ROBIN WAS UNABLE TO TRAVEL WITH ME TO ARUBA when we first received the news about Natalee because her parents, Melvin and Carol Parten, had just left on a cruise and nobody else was available to watch the girls. When they returned from their trip, Melvin and Carol came to stay with our children, and Robin flew in to meet me on June 5, 2005. Later, Robin's brother and sister-in-law, Steve and Leigh Parten, took over the care of the girls. A few days after Robin arrived, my sister, Linda Allison, and my brothers, Steve Holloway and Todd Vestal, also arrived in Aruba to help with our search.

By this time, I was ready to conduct some media interviews. I did not have the energy to stand in front of television cameras every day as some of the others did. I just answered a few questions about my daughter and our search for her and tried to keep my feelings neutral about anything else. Even though I was not happy with the way the authorities were handling the investigation, I saw no reason to make any judgments before completing my investigation. That was just the way I was trained, and I felt that my training had come in handy to keep me moving forward and levelheaded during this time of crisis for all of us. I felt that some publicity might be helpful in getting the word out that

Natalee was missing and asking people to come forward with information, but my time was limited. I knew that if the investigation dragged on, I would have to continue traveling back and forth between Aruba and Meridian for my job. I felt I needed to utilize whatever limited time I had to search for Natalee and meet with authorities.

Approximately six days after Natalee disappeared, two men, Abraham Jones and Antonius Mickey John, former security guards who had worked in a hotel down the street from the Holiday Inn where Natalee was staying, were arrested. Even though there was no sign of Natalee, a judge ruled that there was enough evidence to hold them on suspicion of first and second degree murder, and capital kidnapping, which is kidnapping with intent to do harm or kill. *How could they be accused of murder when we had no idea what happened to Natalee?* I wondered. Apparently, they became suspects when Deepak Kalpoe (one of the boys initially brought in for questioning), told authorities that he, his brother Satish, and Joran van der Sloot had dropped a very intoxicated Natalee off at her hotel and watched as a dark colored man in a black T-shirt with a radio helped her get inside. Little did we know that was only one of many stories the boys would tell about the last night anyone saw Natalee.

While this seemed to be an important development, we were learning more details about Joran van der Sloot that were alarming. He was said to have free run of the island, going where he wanted, drinking, gambling, and telling girls a variety of stories about who he was and where he lived. Apparently, he had even been seen around the casinos gambling right next to his father, Paulus van der Sloot, an attorney rumored to be a judge-in-training on the island. Joran's behavior may not have seemed so unusual except for the fact that he was only seventeen years old, too young to legally be in the casinos or the bars. So far, all we were fairly certain of was that the Kalpoe brothers and Joran were the last ones to be with Natalee, yet they were walking around free.

We also learned that the prime minister of Aruba, Nelson Oduber, had been out of the country in Fort Lauderdale, Florida, when Natalee was reported missing. As soon as he heard about her, he immediately called for Police Chief Jan van der Stratten to be removed from the case and to have the FBI brought in to take charge. Apparently, he did not feel that this was the type of investigation that he wanted to see in van der Stratten's hands. Not having the authority to remove van der Stratten himself due to Dutch rule, the prime minister was frustrated at his inability to take him off the case. At first, some people did not feel comfortable with the FBI getting involved in Natalee's disappearance. Jossy Mansur, editor and owner of the largest newspaper on Aruba, *Diario*, stated, "We do not need the FBI." I am not sure why he felt that way, but during the course of this ordeal, it became clear that Mansur and Prime Minister Oduber had some differences. It was rumored that Mansur's newspaper had allegedly printed statements that Prime Minister Oduber was the most corrupt prime minister Aruba ever had. Prime Minister Oduber brought a lawsuit and supposedly won substantial damages. Mansur eventually did change his mind about having the FBI on the case.

When the prime minister arrived back in Aruba from Fort Lauderdale approximately ten days after Natalee disappeared, his island was inundated with international press members, and he decided that he needed to take action. He must have felt that a meeting with the families would send a clear message that the government was concerned about Natalee. He had previously met with Beth and her family, and it was time to meet with my side. He came to the Holiday Inn with his bodyguard, but the bodyguard did not come into the meeting room—a good faith gesture that this meeting would be private and friendly. His opening remarks were those of a concerned man. He told us that he had a son who was in college, and he expressed his sympathy about Natalee. But then he proceeded to tell us how many hotels he had built and how many other ongoing projects he had. In fact, he said he had a $90 million project currently in the works. He continued rambling, and the family's mood quickly changed, as we were not interested in hearing this kind of self-adulation. We were only concerned about the investigation. I interjected, "Could I have the floor, and can I ask you three simple questions?" The room grew quiet and all eyes were on me. I began my inquiry:

"What is the legal age of gambling?"

"18."

"What is the legal age of alcohol consumption?"

"18."

"What is the legal age of driving?"

"18."

He asked why I wanted to know. I said, "In my country, a judge interprets the law and renders justice based on the crime. He also has the responsibility to project an image to the public that would represent trust, honesty, and integrity. Paulus van der Sloot's son Joran is only seventeen. How can a man training to be a judge sit at a poker table with his son and allow him to gamble, go to Carlos'n Charlie's and order drinks, and even drive? What kind of image does this project upon the average person in Aruba? Ordinary people are fined and sent to prison, but does it apply to Paulus van der Sloot and his son? Are they above the law?"

The prime minister responded, "Nobody here is above the law, and van der Sloot will not be a judge." Apparently, Paulus had failed the test required to become a judge on the island. The prime minister added that he had been trying to close Carlos'n Charlie's for some time. I told him I would quote him and hold him to his word that "No one is above the law."

Suddenly, my brother Phil spoke up. "Natalee has been missing almost two weeks," he said. "I don't like what I have seen as far as the investigation is concerned and where it is going." He raised three fingers, one at a time. As each one went up, he commented, "I can accept finding out that she is not alive. I can accept that she is alive. But if she remains missing, that would not be acceptable based on what has happened in the past ten days. Everything that has happened here is a fiasco!"

The prime minister was taken aback. Phil made it clear that the government needed to do more in the investigation to resolve this case immediately, or he would do everything in his power to bring out the truth about how they had been handling it. I had to step in and call a truce. I did my best to smooth things over, and the meeting ended on a positive note. However, the prime minister may temporarily have had second thoughts about leaving his bodyguard outside of the room.

On June 9, 2005, Joran van der Sloot and Deepak and Satish Kalpoe were finally arrested on suspicion of involvement with Natalee's disappearance. The Kalpoe brothers' home was searched, and the car they were driving the night she vanished was seized. The van der Sloots' home was also searched, and police removed bags of evidence and seized two cars. As far as we knew, nothing incriminating had been found. That was expected since the boys had had plenty of time by then to destroy any evidence. As a matter of fact, we have been told that a witness had watched as they stood in their driveway and scrubbed out their car after police had first questioned them.

While in jail, Deepak supposedly told another suspect, the security guard Antonius Mickey John, that the boys never actually drove back to the Holiday Inn with Natalee. He said that they left Carlos'n Charlie's, drove to the lighthouse, and, on the way back, he and his brother Satish dropped Joran and Natalee off near some fishermen's huts on the beach close to the Marriott Hotel and went straight home. Subsequently, Joran changed his story to match that of the brothers. Looking back, it seems strange that the boy who made the statement that put John and his friend in jail in the first place was now changing his story right to the guy's face. However, it was rumored that he also apologized.

At that point, we still remained optimistic that we would find Natalee. Every day that passed by without finding her allowed us to hold out hope that she was still alive. From the moment I arrived on Aruba, my only plan was to bring her home. I was in a constant search-and-rescue mode. When my body could no longer search, my mind would continue to plan and prepare for the next day. We were lucky to have numerous good-hearted Arubans helping us, along with all of the tourists who had been willing to give up a day at the beach to search. Their efforts truly touched my heart.

We were trying to coordinate our efforts by holding daily meetings with the FBI and police spokespersons. I sometimes felt that those meetings were not very productive. So, after about the third week, I decided that if we were in the middle of a search, I would skip the meeting and get an update over the phone later. Since the meetings were held at 11:00 a.m., I was not going to break up my day by stopping my own search, especially if I was on the other end of the island.

Approximately two and a half weeks into the search, not a clue had been uncovered. Up to this point, the authorities had not been involved in our ongoing efforts to find out what had happened to Natalee. They only agreed to search very specific areas when certain leads came in. For instance, they had just begun to drain the pond by the fishermen's huts in search of a pair of sneakers that Joran van der Sloot had apparently lost in the area on the night Natalee disappeared.

And, while all of this was going on, the Aruban government continued to maintain that their island was safe, but safe for whom? It was obviously not safe for Natalee. There were now five men in custody and absolutely no news about Natalee. Rumors were flying about a reported confession and blood being found in the back of a car. We also heard that one of the boys said that something bad had happened to Natalee and that she had been killed. But none of the stories could be confirmed. Then a radio reporter gave the police information that led them to search the beach near Natalee's hotel. Again nothing was found.

It was hard to know what to believe anymore. The boys' stories kept changing, and the prosecutors in Aruba do not release information the way they do in the United States. All we knew for sure was that the last person to be with Natalee, Joran van der Sloot, had changed his story. First, he said he left her at the hotel, then he said he left her at the beach because she wanted to stay there and that she was fine. Somehow, he expected people, especially Natalee's family, to believe that she asked to be left alone on a deserted beach in a foreign country in the middle of the night. How could anyone accept what he was saying as truth? How many more versions of the truth would he come up with before this ordeal was finally resolved?

On June 13, 2005, the hotel security guards were released from jail after their alibis were verified. We had never really tied them in with the other suspects. There was nothing to indicate that they had been with Natalee or had even seen her. On top of that, the hotel security video did not support the boys' original claims that they had dropped her off there. The only people who we knew for a fact were the last ones to be seen with her were still in jail, and we were grateful for that.

Robin and I were feeling drained. We prayed each day that today would be the day we would find Natalee. We desperately needed to hear what the three boys had to say. We wanted to go and ask them what they did with Natalee, to tell them that we were in agony and that our hearts were broken, and to beg them to reveal to us what they knew. But it was evident that there would be no help from them.

On June 17, 2005, another arrest was made. Steve Gregory Croes, a disc jockey on the tour boat *Tattoo* who had been questioned a few days earlier and released, was now in custody, and the only connection he appeared to have to this case was that he knew one of the Kalpoe brothers from an Internet café. There was no indication that Natalee was ever on the *Tattoo* or anywhere else with this man, but the judge ruled that he could be held for eight days. It was later revealed that Deepak had contacted Croes for an alibi, and Croes later confirmed to police that he had seen the three boys drop Natalee off at the Holiday Inn. What Croes did not realize was that by the time he went to the police with the alibi, Joran had already changed his story. So now Croes's own involvement in Natalee's disappearance was at issue.

On the same day that Croes was arrested, without publicly announcing a reason, a judge ruled that Paulus van der Sloot was not allowed to visit his son, Joran, in jail. We did not know for sure what that was about, but we had strong suspicions that he may have had information about what happened to Natalee. The next day, June 18, 2005, Paulus was brought in for questioning. He was supposedly taken in as a witness.

On June 21, 2005, a search-and-recovery company, led by its director, Tim Miller, volunteered to come to Aruba to join our search. They were comprised of expert searchers from all over the United States, and they brought with them specially trained search dogs and some type of ultrasound equipment that could pick up human remains in the water. They also rented the only helicopter on the island with which to search. Prior to their arrival, my brother Phil, Patrick Murphy, and I had spent about five hours up in the air searching the island for Natalee. Then, after Texas Equusearch's arrival, Tim Miller and I went up two more times to search. Some of the searchers were people who had worked at Fresh Kills Landfill in New York City to look for remains after September 11, 2001. It was incredible to have them all there with us, and we greatly appreciated their efforts.

Shortly thereafter, Joran van der Sloot's mother, Anita, began making public statements to the effect that he had been unfairly targeted. Since we had heard that he had admitted that he was the last one to be seen with Natalee, we felt that the prosecutors were more than justified to "target" him, if, in fact, they had. Mrs. van der Sloot also publicly complained about Joran's visitation restrictions, saying that she could only see her son for ten minutes a day and she was not allowed to talk to him about the crime. She claimed that Joran had only changed his story because he was scared about sneaking out of the house the night Natalee disappeared. Robin and I could only think about how lucky Mrs. van der Sloot was to know the whereabouts of her son. We wondered if she even understood the significance of the fact that Joran had snuck out of the house and then concocted two different stories about his last moments with Natalee before she disappeared. I realize that, as Natalee's parents, we weren't seeing things from Mrs. van der Sloot's point of view, but I can honestly say that if my son was the last person to be with a girl before she went missing and if he had broken our rules by sneaking out and telling lies, I would have interrogated him myself until I got the truth. She had ten days to question him before he was arrested. Instead she defended him. Then she complained about her husband, Paulus, being forbidden by the court from visiting Joran. Robin and I thought there must have been a very good reason for the judge's ruling to keep his father away from him.

On June 23, 2005, two weeks to the day after Joran was arrested, his father, Paulus, was also taken into custody. It was rumored that when the police arrived at the van der Sloot home to arrest Paulus, Anita immediately called Police Chief van der Stratten, who had been under pressure to make an arrest. There was supposedly a problem during the arrest, because Paulus refused to get into the police car. He insisted upon driving himself and that is exactly what he did. A police escort accompanied him to headquarters. I cannot even begin to imagine anyone in the United States, especially an attorney, refusing to go with the police during an arrest and getting away with it. It is not as though Paulus had arranged to surrender himself to the police.

According to an announcement by the prosecutor, Karin Janssen, Paulus was being held on "suspicion of complicity to premeditated murder, complicity to kidnapping and murder and kidnapping." Apparently, he had made statements to the press that conflicted with those he had given when questioned by police. Additionally, there was talk on the island that Paulus had picked his son up early in the morning after Natalee disappeared and knew more than he had admitted. We were pleased with the older van der Sloot's arrest. He should have been brought in sooner, in our opinion; this might be what the three boys needed to push them into a confession.

Meanwhile, the search continued. We did what we could to scour the island, the Aruban government was doing some minimal searching, and Equusearch had the boats and dogs. The Aruban police asked the Equusearch team to send divers into the water that had filled a rock quarry behind the van der Sloot home. Apparently, a body had been found in there many years earlier. We had a meeting with the press and Equusearch, and everyone agreed that only one reporter would be present during this search, but not everyone attended that meeting. Some other members of the news media showed up during the search and were asked to leave, but they refused saying that it was their country and public property. There was a heated confrontation and police had to be called in to rope off the area so the search could continue. The search dogs did not come up with a hit.

We continued to be hopeful that something would finally break in the case. Not a clue had been found, but the lack of evidence did continue to fill us with the hope that Natalee was still alive. We felt certain that those responsible for her disappearance were already in custody and that eventually they would have no choice but to tell the truth.

Our hopes were soon dashed. Two days after his arrest, Paulus van der Sloot was released, as was Steve Croes. Paulus headed for his own car outside of the jail; another indication that he did, in fact, drive there himself. According to the authorities, there was not enough evidence to continue holding them. We felt as though we were on a roller coaster. One minute it looked as though progress had been made, and the next we were back at square one. We'd go three steps forward and one step back, but I did believe that the police were headed in the right direction.

Thankfully, the three boys last seen with Natalee were still in custody, but we could not understand Paulus's release, especially after hearing statements made by Prosecutor Janssen. She said that he had obstructed the investigation early on when he gave the three suspects legal advice before they were arrested. We assumed she was referring to a statement that she said he had made to the boys on the day after Natalee disappeared, "When there is no body, you don't have a case." During questioning by investigators, one of the Kalpoe brothers confirmed that Paulus had said that to the boys.

What kind of a comment is that to make, especially to the last three boys who had seen Natalee alive? We were astonished when we heard that. In our opinion, that implicated him in the crime. We didn't know what part he played other than that he might have done something to protect his son from getting caught. We couldn't even fathom that he might have actually participated in the crime, if, in fact, there was one.

The prosecutor added that Paulus had also summoned one of Joran's friends to his home to find out what he told the police when he was questioned. This was also considered an obstruction. The prosecutor went further, saying that the three boys in custody had been e-mailing and text messaging each other on the night of Natalee's disappearance and that those e-mails and text messages were now in the hands of the police. *What could all of this mean?* we wondered. *Have they found something?*

Apparently, the Kalpoe brothers were now claiming that they had dropped Joran and Natalee off at the beach sometime around 1:30 a.m. and that Joran had text messaged them around 2:40 a.m. to say that he was alone, he had left Natalee on the beach, and he needed a ride home. The Kalpoe brothers claimed they told him that they were already in bed and he should get another ride home. *Another story!* We later learned that there was an eight-minute cell phone call between Joran and the Kalpoe brothers that night, and the prosecutor was investigating what they were talking about for so long.

On July 4, 2005, the unbelievable happened. The Kalpoe brothers were released. The judge ruled that there was not enough evidence to hold them for another sixty days. Joran van der Sloot was to remain behind bars until September 4. Under Dutch law, a suspect can be held on suspicion for 116 days, possibly as long as 146 days, but the judge must grant permission at certain intervals in order for prosecutors to keep someone in custody. There must be a detention hearing after the first 2 days and again at 8-day periods three times. After that, another hearing is held after 60 days and then after the next 30, and again after another 30, if necessary.

When Joran was detained for the sixty-day period, there was also a ruling that he could have daily visits from his family and anyone else, including his father. One day, Robin and I had been out searching and happened upon the prison. I was drenched in sweat, hot, exhausted, and very stressed. My thought was that if Joran was going to continue professing his innocence, he could say it to me face-to-face. His last statement to the police was that he left Natalee at the beach near the Marriott. If he could look me in the eye and just say that he didn't hurt her, I might be satisfied that he was telling the truth. I was hoping that he would also tell me how Natalee was when he left her, her state of mind, her demeanor, her condition, and why she wanted to stay at the beach alone.

I pulled into the prison and went up to the guard shack. The guards informed me that I had to call for an appointment in order to visit a prisoner. The next day, I set up an appointment for that

Saturday. Within a few hours, our attorney received a fax from Joran's attorney saying that Dave Holloway and Beth Holloway Twitty were not allowed to see Joran, but our attorney was unable to reach me directly to inform me of this and so, having no knowledge of this information, I planned to keep the appointment.

After thinking about how I wanted to approach the meeting with Joran, I decided it would be beneficial to bring along an independent witness. During my dinner with the Texas Equusearch team that week, I met Mary Ann Morgan. She claimed to be a psychic intuitive and said she had come to help the Texas Equusearch team. She agreed to accompany me to the prison. I felt that, as an independent observer, another point of view might help me to read the situation more clearly and that I would have an easier time convincing Joran to talk to me with someone else there. I was also hoping to be able to introduce God and the importance of honesty into his life. I obtained a Bible and a book entitled *The Purpose Driven Life* by Rick Warren. I also had a picture of Natalee with her younger sister sitting on her lap. Mary Ann brought a book of her own, entitled *Living in the Moment.* I hoped these things would help me in my pursuit for the truth.

We arrived at the prison at 10:00 a.m. I approached the guard shack surrounded by a number of other guests waiting to see their loved ones. I noticed Paulus van der Sloot, his wife, Anita, a child, and another lady nearby. I approached Paulus and shook his hand. I proceeded to tell him that I had set up an appointment to see his son. I told him that I had heard on television that Joran had continued to profess his innocence. I explained that I requested to see him so he could tell me that face-to-face. I showed Paulus the picture I had of Natalee and her sister and said, "I know where my younger daughter is. However, I don't know where Natalee is. Maybe you could shed some light on this." Paulus's answer to me was that too much time had already elapsed and meeting Joran today would not be possible. Perhaps he felt too much had happened, and he was concerned that Joran's vulnerability in prison might influence him to tell me something incriminating. He also said a meeting might be possible "after the investigation is completed." I wondered what he meant by that statement. He acted as though he already knew what the outcome was going to be. I asked him to discuss with Joran whether he would still consider seeing me. Mary Ann and I left the prison, but decided to return there to see Paulus again when the visitation hour was over.

After an hour had passed, we arrived back at the prison and waited outside. When Paulus and his family exited, I walked up to him and started a conversation. I gripped him with a firm handshake. I wanted to impress upon him how strongly I felt about the situation. Anita spoke up first, saying that Joran was receptive to meeting with me. However, Paulus interjected that we must wait until after the investigation. It was obvious that Paulus did not want me to speak with Joran. *If they are innocent of any crime, why don't they just talk freely with me?* I wondered. *Couldn't Joran at least tell me about Natalee when he last saw her? Couldn't he give me some insight into what might have happened to her?*

I had gone back to the prison for a reason. I wanted to question Paulus regarding his own involvement, if any, in Natalee's disappearance. I don't know why I thought he would tell me the truth, but I hoped his conscience would encourage him to be honest. When I brought up Natalee's disappearance, he immediately stated that he was not involved in any way. I told him that all of the information portrayed about him on TV indicated otherwise, and I began to question him.

"What was Joran's last statement about Natalee?"

"He said he left her at the beach north of the Marriott," he answered. "He said she wanted to stay there. He gave no reason why."

"Why did the boys make up the Holiday Inn story?"

"When Joran and the boys found out that Natalee was missing, they knew they should have taken her back to the Holiday Inn, rather than leaving her at the beach. Joran knew I would be upset, so they came up with this story."

"Why did Joran keep changing his story?"

Joran's mother, Anita, responded to that one: "The interrogators were torturing him."

She later told me that Joran was "probably better off in jail to teach him a lesson." *A lesson for what?* I wondered. She claimed he was innocent. Was she implying that he should be in jail for sneaking out of the house and lying? Wouldn't grounding him have sufficed?

I continued questioning Paulus: "Why did you run from the cameras?"

"I'm not used to media attention."

"Why did it take a four-hour interview with the Dutch reporters from Holland to give a brief statement that really said nothing?"

"The investigation is ongoing, and I did not want to say a lot."

"Why did you say, 'No body, no case?'"

"I did not make that statement. The defense attorney possibly did."

There had been several reports of Paulus making that comment, and it took me by surprise when he denied it. I had heard that statement so many times by then that I was certain that he had said it. I continued questioning him.

"Did you hire the attorneys for the Kalpoe brothers?"

"No, but I gave them a recommendation."

"Are the Kalpoe brothers involved?"

"No."

I wondered how he could be so sure of that. It seemed to me that he should have answered, "I don't know." According to everything he had said, he had no contact with the Kalpoe brothers on the night of Natalee's disappearance.

Anita kept interrupting and interjecting her own thoughts during the conversation. She continued to praise her son and said that the media had blown this whole thing out of proportion.

I decided to ask both Paulus and Anita what the legal ages of gambling, drinking, and driving were on the island. Anita answered that Joran did not gamble and that the tournaments he played in at the casinos did not involve gambling. She also said that the legal drinking age was sixteen and that Joran did not drive because he was only seventeen. I thought it very strange that she did not know the legal age of drinking on the island. Either that, or she didn't think I knew it and she wanted me to believe that it was only sixteen because I knew that her son had been drinking.

Toward the end of our conversation, Paulus noticed a TV camera outside the prison gates and wanted to move toward the guard shack and out of visibility. We finally broke our handshake. It had lasted for about forty-five minutes. The grip had been so tight that Paulus had to move his hand and fingers around to get the circulation back, and my shoulder and arm were sore.

We moved to the sheltered area of the guard station. This is where I took the opportunity to ask Paulus what he really thought had happened to Natalee. He said that we "should look at the Mountain Brook, Alabama, boys. Maybe they did something?" I told him that the FBI had already questioned the students. Paulus then suggested a possible kidnapping. Then, he directed a question at me, asking what I thought had happened to Natalee. I told him that was the reason I was there that day, because I didn't know. I also told him that I did not think there had been an intentional act done against Natalee. I was hoping for some type of response. I added, "I could be a very forgiving person if something happened accidentally." Paulus's eyes began to water, and he told me that he could understand my position. He added, "However, you have to understand that as the father of Joran, I will do everything to protect my son." We then departed.

I knew that he meant what he was saying. I had learned to be skeptical about anything that the van der Sloots and Kalpoe brothers said, but I was sure that Paulus was telling me the truth about doing everything he could to protect his son. I wondered how far he had already gone to keep Joran from being prosecuted.

Leads continued to pour in, and with each and every one of them, Robin and I felt hopeful. Maybe something would turn up that would keep us from having to convert our mission from search-and-rescue to a recovery effort, meaning recovery of a body. It had been so grueling running from one place to the next, watching, waiting, participating, and continuously holding out hope for a clue, a sign, or even a slight indication that Natalee might still be alive. We hadn't found anything of substance to hang on to yet. We were, in effect, in limbo.

As the arrests were being made, we were never really kept informed about what evidence the prosecution may have had, because that was something they did not discuss with us. It is not customary in Aruba to release the details as they do in the United States. We naturally assumed that they must be in possession of some type of incriminating evidence to have made the arrests of all of those suspects. Then, as they released them one after the other, we did not know what to make of it. It was a real disappointment to have our hopes dashed over and over like that. But each time another suspect was released, while Joran remained in custody, we felt sure that prosecutors had something significant against him.

In the middle of July, we thought we finally had some solid evidence. A park ranger found a piece of duct tape with long strands of light and dark blonde hair stuck to it on the beach along the northeast coast. Since Aruba does not have a lab equipped to perform forensic testing, the tape was hand-carried to the Netherlands via the prosecutor, Karin Janssen, and it was also sent to FBI headquarters in Quantico, Virginia, for DNA analysis. A few days later, after having refused to voluntarily give samples, the three boys, Joran, Deepak, and Satish, were summoned to the hospital under a court order to have DNA testing to match up with the duct tape. However, the judge ultimately ruled that the boys' DNA evidence was inadmissible, so none of it was analyzed. However, it was determined that the hair on the tape did not belong to Natalee.

On July 18, 2005, a team of divers found a barrel in the water by the Marriott Hotel, and they, along with several tourists, struggled for hours to pull it up onto the beach. People speculated that it had Natalee's body inside. It turned out to be filled with concrete, and it had been placed there to hold down a buoy. We were incredibly relieved.

Meanwhile, a new witness came forward claiming that he knew where on the island Natalee's body was buried. Texas Equusearch went to the location with equipment that was able to measure ground density to determine if something had been recently buried and a machine to detect vapors from a decomposing body. Nothing was found.

Then, firefighters began draining a pond across from the Marriott Hotel where the Kalpoe brothers claimed to have dropped Joran and Natalee off and where Joran insisted that he left Natalee on the night she disappeared. The draining was sparked by the story of a new witness, a gardener, who came forward saying that, on the night that Natalee had vanished, he had seen all three boys in a car together near the same place by the Marriott where they allegedly left her. The witness said it was around 2:30 a.m., approximately two hours after Natalee left the bar. He claimed to have seen Joran in the driver's seat, Deepak in the front passenger seat, and Satish in the back. They ducked down as if to try to hide from him.

The time was significant because the boys had said they were home by then. The area was searched, but again, nothing was found. However, at the time I didn't know something that I now think is a crucial piece of information: the position that the car was facing when the gardener saw it. If it had been heading away from Carlos'n Charlie's, it would have been on a four-lane highway going past the Holiday Inn on the left. Then, it would have passed the Marriott Hotel on the left, then the lighthouse. Then, it would have passed a dirt road about one hundred yards after the Marriott Hotel on the right cutting across a field. The dirt road is approximately three hundred yards long and leads to the back of the racquet club.

My theory was twofold:

1. If the car was facing the racquet club, then the crime scene was possibly the lighthouse or the beach area north of the Marriott on the left side of road. Joran had supposedly lost his sneakers on the night that Natalee disappeared. Did he lose them while running from the beach and going across the road? The ponds are in an almost direct line, and he may have gotten caught up in some of the surrounding mud. Did the boys take Natalee out of the car and put her in the pond? Hence, there was the reason to drain the ponds.

2. If the car was not facing the racquet club, then the crime scene may have been in the club, in a vacant house that was under

construction around the club, or they were waiting for a rendezvous with another person who would not see the vehicle if it was parked off the roadway. Maybe they were watching the beach area from a distance and out of the way. If the witness was correct, Joran was in the driver's seat, Deepak was in the passenger seat, and Satish was in the back. However, witnesses stated that when they left Carlos'n Charlie's, Joran and Natalee were in the back, with Deepak driving and Satish in the front passenger seat. When and where did they change their seats and why? Were they already planning their alibis? If so, what happened within the approximately one-hour time frame?

Much later, Prosecutor Karin Janssen told me that the car was facing the racquet club next to the pond. Therefore, it had apparently come from the highway that ran adjacent to the Marriott Hotel. By the time she told me about the position of the car, the prosecutor had begun to believe that the boys might never have visited the beach area on the night of Natalee's disappearance.

In the end of July, almost two months after Natalee had disappeared, the pond and field were still in the process of being drained and searched based on the gardener's statement. One pond was drained twice, but the one near where the boys' car was parked the night that Natalee disappeared could not be drained because it was too close to the ocean and the water kept leaching back into it. They had to use heavy equipment to excavate part of the bank, and a helicopter flew over with infrared equipment and detected a heat source in the pond. But, the Texas Equusearch people, using equipment to detect cadavers, determined that it was decomposing shellfish which created a false impression on the infrared.

Another witness, a homeless man who claimed to have been up on the landfill three days after Natalee vanished, said he had seen someone take something out of a pick-up truck that looked like a body and bury it. He described the exact spot with landmarks, but by this time, there had already been a lot of garbage dumped on top of the spot. The searchers dug and came across some of the things the witness said he had seen in the garbage, but they had to use backhoes to dig deeper, and the machinery kept breaking down. We had about forty holes dug and kept sending the dogs down in them. During that entire week, I spent all of my time surrounded by rotting garbage searching for Natalee. It was hot and the stench was so unbearable that we had to wear masks in order to breathe, but we continued to search. My belief was that if we could find the haystack, we could find the needle. *But where is the haystack?* I wondered. *Why can't we find something, anything?*

In the meantime, there were people on the island who believed that Natalee was still alive and running around somewhere having fun in Aruba. They just didn't know her the way we did. I guess with the way the kids on Aruba seem to be allowed to run loose drinking and gambling until all hours of the night, we had to expect that they would perceive her the same way they saw their own kids.

At this point, most of the Equusearch workers had left Aruba, and there were just two searchers still working at the landfill. We requested more searchers and more equipment, and they were coming.

Robin and I still felt very strongly that Joran and the Kalpoe brothers held the key to Natalee's disappearance. They admitted that they were with her, and they kept changing their stories. At the same time, we did not believe that the interrogators were going to be able to break Joran because of the way we understood his father had coached him. Apparently, under Dutch law, the interrogators can withhold food, lie, mislead, and question a suspect for several hours at a time. According to an interview that Anita van der Sloot had with Fox TV's Greta van Sustern, Joran was being subjected to at least ten hours of interrogation a day where he was called a psychopath, a murderer, and a criminal, and had food withheld. The authorities had flown interrogation behavioral specialists in from Holland, and Joran still had not revealed anything. In fact, we heard that he had held his hands over his ears while he was being interrogated.

Paulus told me that he was going to do everything he could to protect his son. As a lawyer, it seemed to me that he would know exactly how—regardless of what that meant for the fate of my daughter.

THREE

Out of Desperation

THE DAYS PASSED BY WITH NO WORD ABOUT NATALEE'S whereabouts. Leads poured in from everywhere. E-mails arrived around the clock with all kinds of suggestions, possibilities, and prayers. I read every one of them. I looked for clues. I grasped at straws. I was desperate. I bloodied my hands from ripping up rocks on the beach in the hopes of finding one tiny shred of evidence. I performed the revolting task of tearing through the contents of a garbage dump in search of my daughter's body. I scoured crack houses looking to see if Natalee was being held captive in one of them. When officials found out that Americans were going into those places and shaking things up, they became infuriated and told me to back off.

I am a father who has no idea what has happened to my child. The questions run through my mind all day long. They keep me awake at night. Is she dead? Is she alive? Is she being held captive somewhere? Are they hurting her? Is she crying out for me? I need to know. I need to find some peace, one way or another.

I wanted to believe that the authorities in Aruba would do everything in their power to find Natalee. I expected them to do that, to comb every grain of sand, search behind every closed door, explore every clue. But they did not begin their investigation early enough, and those first few days are the most crucial. When they should have been following up on every initial lead, suspects could have been out destroying evidence. This did more to frustrate the investigation than anything else. Our family did what we could with everything we had, and it still yielded not a single clue.

Over two months had passed, and the time had come when I had to face the truth. The investigation, the searching, the digging, the air and water searches, in and of themselves, were not producing anything of substance. We were either in all the wrong places or evidence was continuously being moved to keep it one step ahead of us. I had to do more.

Every day, phone calls and e-mails arrived with all sorts of leads and tips. Some seemed to be credible while others appeared to come from people with too much time on their hands. I did my best to try to focus on the most credible, but then I wondered if that was the best way to handle things. What if I was ignoring the one e-mail or phone call that would solve the case and bring Natalee home where she belongs? I admit that my desperation made me participate in things with which I would normally never get involved. But, I had to find out what happened to my daughter. I would have done anything and everything to get to the bottom of this mystery.

Around the beginning of August, Larry Garrison, who has been called the "Newsbreaker," entered the picture. He is president of SilverCreek Entertainment and an executive producer in film and television. He is also a journalist. After spending twenty-five years in network news, he knows how to use the press to his advantage. He had been following our story, and he contacted me to see if there was anything he could do to help find my daughter. I told him about some of the information that people had been sending to us, and he said he would do his best to find a way to investigate anything relevant. He sifted through the tips and took some of our most plausible leads to networks like ABC News, NBC News, MSNBC News, and others and asked their investigators to follow up on them. Some of the stories that Larry has given them include the following two:

- Approximately one week after Natalee's disappearance, a decapitated man was found in a local Aruba cemetery. I do not think his death was reported in any local news stories. Rumor has it that the man was in charge of incinerating bodies at the nearby funeral home. Some speculate as to whether this man may have been hired by Paulus van der Sloot to incinerate Natalee's lifeless body and was then murdered to keep him quiet. It is more than I can bear to think of Natalee that way. Unfortunately, no connection has yet been made to Natalee's disappearance.

- An e-mail came in stating that the authorities had found a key in Deepak Kalpoe's car but that the police chief lost it. The key supposedly allowed access to an old underground kitchen in the basement of the former Wyndham Hotel. According to the e-mail, Deepak's mother may have worked there and the boys may have used the kitchen as a hiding place. The tip also suggested that there is a cooler in the kitchen that might contain Natalee's body. We were hoping the investigators that Larry contacted could use the information about the key to find answers. However, ABC News investigated the situation, and nothing evolved from it.

Some tips require my participation in order to uncover the truth. If a meeting is requested that I must attend and the person asking for it seems fairly credible, I am willing to take a chance and be present. One such situation demanded my personal attention.

On Thursday, June 9, 2005, a gentleman from Houston, Texas, left a message on my hotel phone indicating that he had new technology that could locate human bodies. He said he was arriving in Aruba later that evening and wanted to meet with me.

The gentleman from Texas called my hotel room a second time that day. He had already checked into the Holiday Inn and brought his technology with him. Another call came from a man who lived in Aruba. He identified himself as a Mason and told me that the gentleman from Texas, also a Mason, had contacted him to act as a liaison. He then told me there was something special about the Masons. It was too late in the evening, and I was too tired to be impressed, so I told him to call me back in the morning. He called the next day to tell me that the Texan was in the lobby of my hotel. I told him we would be right down to speak with him. My brothers, Phil and Todd, and my brother-in-law, Michael, followed Robin and me down to the lobby.

The Texan appeared to be in his seventies. The Aruban, a younger man around thirty, told me that the Texan had brought with him new technology that could locate human bodies. All he needed was a hair sample. I was somewhat skeptical, and my skepticism only increased when he pushed again for a sample of Natalee's hair. I was not about to give just anyone something so personal. How did I know that this was not a ploy to get his hands on something to sell on eBay or keep as a souvenir or use as an opportunity to simply brag that he had a piece of my daughter's hair? But I had to get to the bottom of this, and, in truth, I was curious about what his machine could really do.

He continued to ask for the hair, and I told him that Beth, my ex-wife, had the sample and that I would need more information and a demonstration before I would even consider getting the hair for him.

Phil, Todd, and Michael accompanied the Aruban, the Texan, and me to the Texan's room. Inside, I was handed a research booklet and résumé that mentioned his invention. I was told that his technology referenced "DNI," which the Texan said was more accurate than DNA. The man told us he was an engineer and had performed a lot of research and created many inventions. We discussed his purpose for being there and why he was interested in locating my daughter at his own expense. He did have an ulterior motive. He wanted to prove to the Department of Defense that his technology worked, and he believed that solving this case would get their attention. He had already proposed it to NASA and the Defense Department, and they did not take him seriously. He claimed that this technology, if placed on military vehicles in Kuwait, would detect bombs. I thought it odd that he mentioned Kuwait rather than Iraq considering that the United States was fighting a war in Iraq at the time. However, I did not question his comment.

Time was wasting. "Let's see your technology," I insisted. The Texan walked over to the corner of the room and picked up a large suitcase. He carried it to the bed, laid it down, and opened it. Inside was another case. He pulled it out. By now, my mind was racing. *What is in it?* I wondered. When he flipped open the lid, I saw a device with two white cylinder-shaped objects with two red rings around them. It was round and oblong and approximately six inches in diameter by ten inches long. It looked radioactive. There was a sharp steel rod at the bottom, which the Texan said would be used to stick in the ground. There were also wires on the top. The Texan explained that they would be placed into the ground approximately six inches apart. *Okay, there is obviously something missing. Where is the rest?* I wondered. I was about to leave when he pulled out the other part. I could tell that the rest of the group was still interested, so I remained where I was.

The other part consisted of two rods that were approximately two feet in length. The end made a ninety-degree angle and was approximately six inches long with swiveled handles attached. It resembled dousing rods. The Texan again requested Natalee's hair. He said he really needed it now. I demanded to know how the machine worked first. He pulled out some copper and placed it between the white pods that stood up in the corner of the room. Then, he walked to the other side of the room and, while holding the swiveled handles that were on one end of the rods, he asked us to watch the other end of the rods. He said that the white pods on the opposite side of the room would pick up the DNI in the copper sample and then transmit that through to the rods he was holding. That would cause the rods to point to the copper sample that had been placed on the other side of the room. I was watching his hands closely while everyone else was fixated on the end of the rods. With an almost unnoticeable tip of his hands, the rods miraculously turned toward the copper. Jaws dropped and eyes opened wide. I was not amused as I saw what had actually occurred. The next demonstration was with, of all things, a sample of his very own wife's hair. Again, no one caught on but me. His wife was not even there. He was going to use two locks of her hair, one in the machine and one on the other side of the room where the machine would detect it. I was not surprised at what happened next. He had made the rods swing with a slight movement of the handles. The swivels on the other end balanced the rod. The hand movement had caused the rod to turn toward the wife's hair.

I jokingly questioned why, with such a great invention, he did not own all the gold and diamonds in the world. He then quipped that he was a millionaire and did not need the money. By this time, Phil and Michael were suspicious. Another demand came for Natalee's hair. I told the Texan that all I may be able to get would be a few strands. He assured me that would be sufficient.

"Wait a minute," I said. "We are in a small room. This search would take years on an island this large, approximately five miles by twenty miles."

"Oh, no," said the Texan. "This machine will pick up things at a distance of at least six miles." He said he would only need about three areas to set up: one near the top of the island, one in the middle, and the other at the bottom. "Now, let's get the hair!"

My wife, Robin, had been with us at the beginning of our conversation in the lobby, and she had stayed behind to get Natalee's hair sample from Beth. Now I was concerned that she would show up with the hair, and I did not want her to do that. I felt that we had been duped, and I wanted to get out of there. I had to find a way to convince the others that we needed to leave. We were wasting valuable search time. I thought fast. I quickly reached up to the top of my head and jerked out a few strands of my own hair. I wanted to see if he could make the machine work on me. "No problem," he casually commented. He gave me a plastic bag to put the hair in, and I put the sample between the white pods. He set the test up and told me to walk across the room. I suggested, "Better than that, if the machine can pick up something six miles away, I'll just walk out of the room and go down the hall." My brother Todd stood at the door to let the Texan know when I was ready. I had whispered to Todd to look in the opposite direction from where I was standing in order to keep the Texan from knowing where I really was. Todd looked to his left and called down the hall to ask me if I was ready. The Texan saw him glance to the left and the rods suddenly turned that way. Todd told him he was wrong. The Texan made up an excuse. They wanted one more chance. Todd and I did the same set-up scenario, but Todd glanced to his right this time and asked if I was ready. I was actually standing right behind him out of sight. Once again, the rods went in the direction that Todd had glanced.

I told the man that I was sorry he had spent his money and taken his time to come here, but I would not be able to get a hair sample for him. I would discuss what had happened with Beth and, if she agreed, she could talk to him. I took my hair back and left.

Our timing was perfect. As we exited the man's room, Robin was rushing down the hall with Natalee's hair sample. I asked her to return it to Beth and tell her it was a hoax.

Later in the day, we saw the Texan sitting in the lobby. I spoke with him, and he told me he would be there until Tuesday. I told him that Beth had been informed about what had happened with the test and that we were no longer interested.

I never did learn what his real intentions were. I almost think he was lost in time . . . talking about Kuwait in 1991. I truly felt sorry for the man. He really did believe in himself. Unfortunately, we did not. It was time to move on and investigate another lead.

Someone from the Aruban prime minister's office called my sister, Linda. The caller claimed that a man told him that he wanted to meet with me because he thought the situation with Natalee was hurting Aruba's economy. The prime minister's office arranged for Linda and me to meet with the man, a Buddhist who wanted to remain anonymous, at a place called the VIP Club. Linda was nervous about the meeting and went ahead of us to scope out the place with a reporter, Craig Rivera, and his cameraman, Greg. It was located on the highway, and it looked like a sleazy strip club. The windows were blackened, and there was only limited parking out in front. It was connected to an Indian or Chinese restaurant, and there was a seedy looking motel next door separated by a narrow road. After seeing all of that, Linda was skeptical. But we decided to go ahead with the meeting. What did we have to lose . . . except time?

We were running late from a prior engagement, and we had media following us. We were forced to double back in order to lose them. When we arrived at the place, I saw that it was right in the middle of a main thoroughfare. The building was dark, as was the parking lot. The scenario was quite unsettling. However, we felt somewhat safe because Craig and his cameraman had agreed to wait outside in case we got into trouble. Craig wanted to wire us, but I said no. Instead, Linda programmed his number into her cell phone, and she planned to hit it if we needed help or felt that we wanted Craig to hear what was going on.

We were nervous, but we reluctantly followed a man who had come outside to get us. He led us down a dark alley along the side of the building. There was nothing but tall brush and cactus on the right-hand side, and my fear was that with the man ahead of us and the building and cactus on either side, someone could come up behind us, and we would be trapped. We were even more apprehensive now. When we got around to the back of the building, the man opened a door leading into a dimly lit conference room. We hesitantly walked through that into an office. There, we met another man who looked like he was from India. He introduced himself as a doctor and a Buddhist medium. He explained that he was a wealthy man and wanted nothing from us. He also made it clear that he did not want publicity. He just wanted to help the island get over this terrible incident, and he also wanted to help us in our search for Natalee.

The man started out by telling me information: "You are searching endlessly for your daughter."

What an intuitive, I laughed to myself.

He continued, "When they say she is in the east, she is in the west." Then he began to ask questions: "What is Natalee's date of birth?"

I didn't answer him; I was not going to give him any personal information about her.

Again, he spoke. "I know that you have been divorced for about ten years."

I corrected him. It had been twelve.

"You have two children."

"No, I have more."

"You like to go fishing."

"I haven't gone fishing for about ten years."

"You have a lot of money."

"No, I don't. I'm very far in debt. Maybe you're thinking about the other side of the family."

"You have a scar on your back."

"No, I don't."

"Does Natalee have a scar on her back?"

"No."

"Does Natalee have a red mole under her arm?"

"No."

I became concerned with all of the personal questions. I began asking myself what was really happening here. Was this a kidnapping attempt? Would we be able to leave here alive? At this point, I knew it was time to get out of there. Linda pushed the button on her phone so that Craig could hear the scam going on. Thankfully, we were able to just walk out.

We later learned from Craig that these scam artists play on

others' emotions when a tragedy strikes, then they leave them hanging on the edge. They ask for money to proceed with helping them through their ordeal. I suppose that some people are so desperate they fall into the trap. Thankfully, I have not yet succumbed to that scheme.

On a later trip to Aruba, I told Detectives Eric Soemers and Dennis Jacobs about the Buddhist my sister and I had met at the VIP Club. They seemed to know who he was and said he is a psychic. Then, they drove me to see the motel next door to the VIP Club. I was told it was a whorehouse where you pay by the hour. I did not know if that meant you bring your own girl or they furnish one.

The motel has a small home-like structure at the front. Then, there are six or seven rooms that stretch down the roadway. There were no vehicles there during daylight, but we heard that some young girls were escorted in and out of the rooms that day. We had also heard that someone had arrived that day with sophisticated camera equipment. There is reason to believe that the Buddhist who met me and my sister next door at the VIP Club may have known the person or persons who were holding Natalee captive in the motel and was trying to make a deal to sell her back to me. The authorities were supposedly investigating this. As with most of the leads that we had turned over to police, nothing ever evolved from it. We also heard that this might be the place where a friend of Joran's, Freddy Alexander Zedan-Arambatzis, was alleged to have taken lewd pictures of a minor girl. He has denied the charge, but his lawyer says he admits he was present when photos of the girl in "tempting poses" were taken.

The detectives knew the motel's owner, so we drove by his home. We were hoping he would be there so we could talk to him. We were in an unmarked car with heavily tinted windows and a regular license plate that was rotated out frequently so as not to be recognizable. He was not at home, but the detectives said they would keep a close watch on him.

As a Christian man, it is hard for me to give credence to psychics. That type of so-called phenomena is outside the realm of my faith. However, I never imagined this type of tragedy hitting my family. So when I met Mary Ann Morgan, the psychic who said she had come to Aruba to help the Texas Equusearch team, I was willing to listen to what she had to say. She claimed that Natalee had contacted her and had given her messages for Beth and me. She told me that she had "conversations" with my daughter and some of her details seemed so obscure that I wondered how she could have known them. She said that Natalee told her what happened the night she disappeared. According to her, Natalee said that the boys gave her a date rape drug, took her out to the lighthouse area, then to Joran's apartment where Joran had choked her. The boys arranged to put her body in a solid white fish container that fit at the rear of the fishing boats, weighed it down, and took her out to sea. Since there were already reports of a cage being stolen from one of the fishermen huts, along with speculation that Natalee had been taken out to sea in it, the search took place.

The Texas Equusearch team took the information and had their divers go into the sea at the northeast side of the island for several days, but they could not find anything. The sea was so rough that everyone except the captain got seasick. They made approximately three futile attempts to dive. It was finally a forensic team of scuba divers from Florida State University who cleared the area after Mary Ann gave them the coordinates. No trace of evidence was found.

Mary Ann said that, as a psychic, she does not get emotionally involved in cases, but she did so this time. She claimed that she had become so concerned about Natalee that this may have had an effect on her ability to solve the case. One of the things she could not explain was a statement that Natalee supposedly made to her that she was buried in the sea "by the work they do." Later, she contacted me saying that she thought that the seaport and Yacht Basin located near Carlos'n Charlie's and the Internet cafe might hold the answer, as Deepak is the only one who works. She felt that the comment "by the work that they do" could only relate to him. Mary Ann gave us some clues as did all of the other psychics who contacted us, but the jury is out until she finds my daughter.

Another unusual experience that we had came from a man who contacted us claiming to have sent a DVD to my ex-wife, Beth, in Alabama. He detailed how he had a confession from Joran van der Sloot's father, Paulus, on the DVD and said that Beth had not yet picked up his proof from the post office. I asked Larry Garrison to follow up on this one by calling him. The man was sleeping, and his wife had to drag him out of bed to speak with Larry. He claimed to have technology that proved that Joran's father said on national television that he kidnapped and killed my daughter. He then exclaimed that his technology was so technical that if it fell into the wrong hands, the president and mankind would be in jeopardy. At that point, Larry thought this guy was going to be added to the list of certifiably insane people. Out of curiosity, Larry asked for him to send his DVD. The man and his wife promised to express it the next day.

More than a week went by, and we realized that he had never sent it. Out of curiosity, Larry e-mailed the man asking about the DVD. This was his response:

> I still don't know who you are? What you do? But I am a man of my Word and I did say I'd send you a copy . . . so I will . . . are you in Law

Enforcement? A Lawyer? P.I. or what? Why are you so interested in the Technology? Or is it just the Money? I told you that I've sent copies to Jug & Beth Twitty . . . They're giving up! Joran and his dad has gone to Holland . . . in Beth's words . . . We've Exhausted all our avenues here in Aruba." They have spent alot I suppose . . . and have Trusted in alot of differant people or organizations to help them! They've tried everything . . . Body Analysis—Stress Analysis guys—and, have dug up ponds and trash dumps . . . I was the first to Varify that Natalee had been Murdered . . . and "It came from the Mouths of Paul and Anita VanDer Sloot. . ." I was the first to Offer the Best Lead as to where her Body was . . . Again NOT MY WORDS—but from the Mouths of the VanDer Sloot's. Oh— You're gonna hear it . . . I'm gonna mail you the DVD—in fact I may go a step further and send you several cases—Would you like to know WHO Killed Jonbenet Ramsey? I'm mean—Confessions . . . I don't know you . . . and Yes I am a Christian . . . I don't have time to [BS] around . . . and I don't waste my time on people who "Have a form of Godliness . . who say, I'm a Christian—or Hang a Big Cross around their neck and say We Pray for the Truth . . . but deny the Power thereof" . . . Anyway . . . you Watch and you Listen Real Close . . . and you tell me the source of what you hear and see! Do with it what you will . . .They're on the way . . . Tomorrow . . . Saturday, 09.10.05 . . . In The Master's Service."

One week later, we received the DVD. The package was small and upon opening it, a letter dropped out. The writer claimed that the technology was registered with an attorney. We put the DVD into our computer hoping that it would either be constructive or, at the very least, provide some interesting entertainment. What we viewed was both fascinating and ridiculous. The screen immediately opened up to a globe of the world. In the next frame in bold black letters it read, "TRUTH." Then, it cut to the president of the United States speaking about the judicial system. At the top of the screen was written the name of the man's company. There were also various news clips on Natalee and some of the family speaking to the press. In one clip, he had Jug Twitty, Beth's husband, supposedly saying, "We hope the Aruban Government uses this resource," as if to make it seem as though Jug is actually promoting this guy's technology. The screen then opened up to a "Barney Fife of Mayberry"-type security guard dressed in a uniform. He introduced himself and explained that Israel uses similar technology with online truth communications. He continued, saying that lie detectors are not admissible in a court of law, but his technology has never been questioned as to its effectiveness. He said that lie detectors work on the nervous system, while his technology uses the human voice. He stated, "This new technology reveals a person's subconscious thoughts, and the Lord has created the brain which has embedded these thoughts for analysis. With the use of a computer, one can slow up or speed up speech and also run it backwards." That's right, backward, and that is what he did to get to what he called the truth. Next, there are about twenty-four minutes of clips showing the security guard at the hotel, Anita van der Sloot, Paul van der Sloot, and others. The most interesting part of the DVD was that somehow it showed people saying they had killed Natalee. Also, Anita's words were reversed and translated so she was speaking backward, and we could hear her saying that Natalee was buried in a cemetery on top of a family member or friend whom she named. Though it all seemed outrageous, I decided to leave no stone unturned and gave the clue to the investigators. No big surprise, the tape proved to be useless to us.

Another man sent me a long and very intricate report claiming to have a method that allows "trained profilers to analyze a suspect's verbal statements to identify and understand subtle instances of subconscious confession." In other words, he can read between the lines of a suspect's statements and body language to determine what the person really knows about a crime. His conclusion was that Natalee had been drugged and raped by the boys and that she died during the sexual assault. He also said that it is likely that Paulus van der Sloot was involved in disposing of Natalee's body, most likely in the ocean or on the island. The researcher said that his report could be used as circumstantial evidence. I read through his very extensive report and spoke to him, and he told me that he never actually talked to the boys but used excerpts from the Internet and some of the statements that had leaked out. It would be difficult, in my opinion, to come to a valid conclusion without all of the boys' statements and without being present during any of the questioning or interviews. It is another good theory—maybe even a likely scenario—but I believe that he would need all of the information to make an accurate judgment. And he didn't have that.

On one particular trip to Aruba in September 2005 to continue with my search and meet with my attorney, Vinda De Sousa, and Prosecutor Janssen, I followed a lead that had come in from another psychic. The person had never been to Aruba, but somehow managed to describe the terrain and direct me to a well where Natalee was supposedly buried. I arrived there to find a well with twigs all over it and stones thrown down inside. I could not go down into it myself, but a fireman did, and he confirmed that nothing was down there. It was just another false lead, but I had to check it out.

On that same trip, my father-in-law, Melvin Parten, accompanied me at 5:30 a.m. to the island's bird sanctuary. This was where it had been reported that the cadaver dogs had some hits, but it was unclear whether it had been thoroughly searched. It is twenty acres of waist-high stagnant water and lily pads, which we walked through for over three hours looking for clues about Natalee. We did not realize that the water would be so deep and that the roots of the lily pads would obstruct our efforts to cross or search the water. Not only would the lily pads obstruct our search, but we also realized that they were strong enough to hold a body down, which made searching the area much more tedious. Climbing up the bank onto the grass was very difficult. Our attempts to go through the grass were almost impossible, and we felt that if someone were carrying 105 pounds, they could not have gone very far. We waded around for over three hours until the fatigue and heat set in. We knew we needed more help to clear this area. I remembered hearing that Joran had lost his sneakers near McDonalds, which is right next door to the sanctuary. I almost lost my own shoes walking through the mud, so I believe that Joran's sneakers may be in there.

When my father-in-law and I were finished searching, the stench on us was so bad that we had to take the floor mats from the car and put them on the seats to sit on. We drove straight to the ocean and jumped in to clean the sewage off before going back to wash our clothes. We had to wash them twice to get the smell out.

Out of desperation, I cannot ignore any of the information that people send about Natalee. I take the initiative as much as I can to investigate the leads myself, but when I cannot, I hand them over to family members, friends, and others who have been kind enough to help me search for information about Natalee. It is incredible how many people insist they know what happened to her. I hang on to the hope that one of them will be right.

Every once in a while, I try to stand back and take a few moments to separate myself from the situation to make sure that I have not lost my objectivity or my sanity. I do not want to delve so deeply into the fantasies of well-meaning individuals that I lose my footing and slip out of reality. Someone once said that insanity is a perfectly rational adjustment to an insane world. Right now, I can relate to that thought. It is a fine line that I walk to stay on the side of rational thinking in the face of all of the con artists and out-landish schemes that I have been exposed to since Natalee's disap-pearance. The hope that I have for finding out what happened to my Natalee is what keeps this desperate father from allowing the torment and agony to overwhelm me to the point of distraction. I maintain an open mind, but I scrutinize every tip. I am careful not to accept the incredulous before a thorough examination takes place. However, I have learned to hold aside some room in my belief system for the inconceivable.

It is time to go now. Someone is claiming to be able to find Natalee with a Doppler over water.

FOUR

Following the Trail

ROBIN AND I WERE FRUSTRATED. IT WAS AUGUST AND Natalee should have been preparing to go off to college soon, her birthday was coming up, and we still had no idea what had happened to her. It seemed impossible that she had just disappeared without a trace. We held on to our belief that God was there with us to guide us, and we continued to pray for the strength to get through another day.

Prime Minister Oduber had brought the FBI into Natalee's case early on, but they had no authority to do anything except act in an advisory capacity. They were not even allowed access to any case records. In late July, the prime minister had asked the attorney general to allow them to be given "complete access to the dossier, including transcripts, audiotapes or video registration of interrogations, plus all materials that are connected to this case, in as much as our judicial system allows." Joran's attorney made a motion to the court to forbid the FBI from having access to the files. Thankfully, the judge rejected the motion, and the FBI was allowed to see them. Robin and I were very encouraged by the ruling. We were hoping that their input would make a substantial difference in the case, especially with the current feeling among some of us that there might have been a cover-up by Aruban authorities that wanted the whole mess swept under the rug.

We were not the only ones who were happy to have the FBI in on the case.

On MSNBC, Jossy Mansur told Rita Cosby, "I think if . . . they didn't elect to have the FBI . . . involved, then everyone should boycott Aruba because the FBI should have been brought in in the beginning into this case. It was a case of a missing American woman. And I've worked cases with Scotland Yard and Interpol. Countries have used each other's resources. And I know that the Aruban police were not experienced in cases of missing women, and the FBI should have been asked in right from the beginning to help them interrogate this guy and those two brothers that they let out of jail. So it's crucial that the FBI be involved, if only for their . . . ability to do forensics."

By then, Mansur had become a major player in the case, especially involving the media attention surrounding Natalee. He also appeared to have an enormous amount of influence on the island. He seemed to know everything that was happening even before most others, and he did not hesitate to report it. For example, he publicly announced that Joran van der Sloot had a reputation on the island for drinking, gambling, and even dropping pills into girls' drinks. He also reported that "there were two more involved in the disappearance of Natalee Holloway. One drove a white truck while the other apparently dumped Natalee Holloway into the landfill." Mansur also brought forward the landfill witness who said he saw people burying a body, and he was responsible for bringing in the backhoes to dig at the landfill to look for it.

I heard that he had informed some members of our family that drug dealers had kidnapped Natalee and that they were holding her for a $10,000 ransom. Family members met with the drug dealers, and subsequently they were notified that the police had rescued a girl who they were "98 percent" sure was Natalee. However, at the police station, they found that the woman police rescued did not look anything like Natalee and was about forty-five years old.

Mansur also brought in Art Wood, a former Secret Service Special Agent from Florida, who uncovered some very important clues and was responsible for finding the gardener whose statement contradicted those of the three main suspects. Unfortunately, the gardener did not show up for court, and it was alleged that he had fled the island because he was there illegally. However, he was finally located, and he repeated his statement to the police as well as to the court that he had seen the three suspects in the field next to the pond long after they claimed to be home. Mansur also came forward with information that he knew of three women who claimed to have been date raped by Joran van der Sloot. And he was the one to break the news that Joran confessed to the police on the second day of interrogations as a suspect that "we buried Natalee." Former FBI profiler Clint van Zandt claimed to have seen the reported confession that was allegedly given in the presence of four Aruban police officers. Van Zandt added that Joran accused Deepak of sexually assaulting, murdering, and burying Natalee.

On Fox News, Mansur first confirmed that the boy who had allegedly taken pictures of the minor girl at the motel, Freddy Alexander Zedan-Arambatzis, had been arrested, the details of which will be discussed shortly.

While on CNN's *Headline News* with Nancy Grace, Mansur claimed to have a picture of Joran wearing brown boots at Carlos'n Charlie's on the night that Natalee disappeared. His statement was meant to dispute the claim that Joran lost a pair of blue and white tennis sneakers that night. However, he later acknowledged that he had been mistaken about the picture. It had been taken a couple of months before Natalee was in Aruba.

We didn't really know why Mansur had become such a vocal advocate for our cause. There were all sorts of rumors, but he finally answered our question. On an airing of MSNBC's *Abrams Report*, Mansur was asked why he was involved in Natalee's case. He responded,

> I am involved for many reasons. Number one, I feel a strong affinity to this Alabama family that came here. I studied in Alabama. I went to college in Mobile, Alabama. I also went to high school in Mississippi, so I do feel a strong affinity to them. I know the people of those two states were very nice people to me when I was there at school, always invited on any holiday to one family or another's home for Easter or Christmas or whatever, and I found them to be very fine and very classy people. . . . The reason is she is an American girl, a U.S. citizen that's disappeared from our island, and it's up to us, every single Aruban, to contribute and help and do whatever is necessary to find her . . . and we have our contacts also here locally that we've built over 25 years, so we have access to certain information no one else has.

There is no disputing that Mansur's publicity has kept Natalee's face a visible focus on Aruba for a long time. He continues to be an advocate for our cause.

By the beginning of August, I had already spent at least fifty days in Aruba, and it was wearing me thin. While reports were coming from people like Jossy Mansur and others, I was quite depressed about the lack of any solid information in Natalee's case. There were moments when we desperately needed to regroup, but we had to keep moving forward in our search for Natalee. During those times when we traveled back home, life was a little easier, because being with friends and family put us back into our comfort zone and made the days more bearable. It was hard to take, when we reflected on college and her birthday and then pictured Natalee being buried in a landfill or at sea. It was during those times that I would take a moment to reflect back to when Natalee was much younger. I suppose we all do that when our children leave home. We wish for those times when we still have them under our wings, knowing their every move, and watching them learn about life. But, this is different from anything I had envisioned. I had planned to someday tell Natalee's children about her growing up years, as she would sit nearby giggling and correcting me and telling it her own way. I would be showing them pictures of their mother from when she was their age. I never imagined that I would be describing to the world what my missing daughter was like, the pride that we felt sharing her accomplishments, the joy she brought to us, and the terrible pain we are in now. It isn't easy not knowing how the story will end. So I continue to take my little trips back in time to be with Natalee again and to remember how happy we once were. Although I had always cherished our memories, it is only now that I realize how very important they really are to me. Each moment with Natalee, each smile, each hug, each "I love you, Daddy" has been a blessing, and they help to sustain me during this agonizing journey. I can close my eyes and still hold on to my little girl, if only for a fleeting instant.

When Natalee was young, I had to come up with at least two bedtime stories each night, and sometimes a third one when I was on a roll. This ritual continued every other weekend for many years. Most of those stories were told over and over again, with a little extra spice added each time. Natalee's favorite was the "Bear" story.

The basis for the bear story was a true event that happened when I was a young boy. Natalee and Matt could relate, because I was telling it from a perspective that matched their age group. I grew up in rural Arkansas, and we had a black bear that would visit our garbage can every now and then. After every visit, we would have to clean up the garbage from the backyard area. We initially thought it was a stray dog, so, after securing the garbage can by covering the lid with a large rock, we felt our troubles were over. One hot summer night, my older brother decided to sleep on the couch next to the window unit. He was awakened by the rustling of something in the garbage can and decided to turn on the back porch light. He was surprised to see a bear looking up at him. The bear then barreled off down the hill. My brother went back to sleep and waited until the next day to tell us about it. When we heard about the bear, we decided to use honey to attract him back again. This was the point where the story took off to whatever my mind could imagine. I used different scenarios to create a new story each time. I would tell the basic story and after the honey, I would make up some far-fetched ending, such as that the bear tried to break into our house, or that the bear would run away and come back, and how he would growl at us and we would be scared. Natalee and Matt loved hearing the stories over the years, and I had as much fun telling them.

The other tales I told them came from their storybooks. After the stories, our last thing at night was to pray to God. Natalee and Matt were taught to do it the traditional way, kneeling in front of their beds with their hands together. This meant so much to them growing up. They took their faith very seriously. In fact, one year we had a tornado warning, and during the storm, Natalee and

Matt ran into their bedrooms, grabbed their Bibles, and started praying. They knew who was watching over them . . . besides Robin and me.

We also did a lot of camping in northern Arkansas. We would pull our travel trailer to a camping area along the Spring River and spend several days floating the river, fishing, and doing fun kid stuff. The nights around the campfires brought more stories. However, those usually involved a practical joke rather than a bear. One of the adults would slip off and hide. While a scary story was being told, the adult would make some noises in the distance or in the area behind the kids. The noise and brush crunching would get closer and closer until the adult would disclose their identity by rushing out into the campfire circle. The kids would scream and laugh, and we all had a great time.

Our trips to Natalee and Matt's grandmother's house always had to include a trip through a small graveyard that had a circle drive. We would sometimes stop and roll down the windows to see if we could hear or see anything. As the years passed, we would coax someone to be in the graveyard to walk around and make believe it was haunted. Finally, in later years, Natalee, Matt, and their cousins would be the ones trying to pull something over on the younger kids. One year, they adorned Halloween masks, and another time they wore white sheets to appear as ghosts that arose from a grave.

We always did things as a family. We went to a number of football games, parks, beaches, and anything else we could do together. Sunday was our church day, and as a prerequisite to coming to stay for the weekend, Natalee and Matt had to have their church clothes packed when they were picked up on Friday evenings.

As Natalee got older and obtained her driver's license, I could see that our time would be shared with her close friends and her activities in school and in her life. She was growing up and, though it was an adjustment, it was also a time of joy. She was turning into a beautiful young woman.

As I reflected on those precious memories, I was suddenly pulled back to reality. Natalee had gone to Aruba. She was missing, and I couldn't bear the thought of what may have happened to her. I wanted desperately for her to be alive, but what if she was? Was she being held captive by one of those sex slave rings that I heard about? There were many stories coming back to me about places where girls are kept and drugged and forced to work as prostitutes on islands in the area surrounding Aruba. For instance, one woman had been talking on the phone with her sister during a storm and the lines got crossed. She found herself listening to a conversation between two men who were talking about Natalee. One of the men said he had gone to a brothel in Bogotá, Colombia, and saw a girl who worked there that looked like Natalee. The other man asked if he was going to give the information to the FBI. The man responded that he works in Washington, and he was afraid of what his family would say if they found out that he had been to a brothel. The woman listening in also said that it was clear from the conversation that men in high places, like politicians, frequent the brothel.

Another story about sex slavery came to us from a woman whose husband grew up in Meridian, Mississippi, where Robin and I live. She and her husband have a friend who was a sailboat captain around Aruba, and he still traveled back there occasionally. The friend passed on information to me saying that I should investigate what goes on in Curacao and the small islands around it. Apparently, he had taken many people to and from the area, and he was told that there are houses of prostitution where the Curacaos keep girls who are so drugged up that they don't know who or where they are. But he warned me to be careful with the information, because if they were to become suspicious that any-one found out where they were, they will move somewhere else. He had been in and out of the islands so often over the years that he became friends with the locals. They trusted him enough to show him the houses so he saw this himself. He believes that Natalee is being held in one of those houses and that the Kalpoe brothers and Joran sold her. There are people who have been scouring known brothels on the islands around Aruba for Natalee.

His story is not far-fetched. It is reminiscent of one that I have heard about since Natalee has been missing. A twenty-three-year-old girl named Amy Bradley was reported missing on March 24, 1998. She had been on a cruise with her family en route to Curacao. By the time the boat had docked, she was gone. Subsequently, a cab driver in Curacao told Amy's father that he had seen her on the morning that she had disappeared and that she had told him she needed to get to a phone. Another person, a U.S. Navy Petty Officer, reported having seen Amy in a Curacao brothel. He said she asked him for help and told him her name. He did not report the incident when it happened because he was afraid that he would get into trouble with the Navy for going to a brothel. He waited until he retired and saw a story about her before he contacted her family to tell them what he had seen.

Amazingly, there were three men on Amy's cruise ship who had tried to convince her to go with them to Carlos'n Charlie's. Her parents are sure that someone was able to get her off the ship as it was docking in Curacao without anyone noticing.

On June 8, 2005, CNN *Headline News* with Nancy Grace had as a guest Debra Opri, the Michael Jackson family attorney. When asked her opinion on Natalee's disappearance, she answered, "I do believe, if they follow the leads they've gotten, or including the forensic evidence, it may lead to . . . Aruba being a way station for some sort of activity in drugs or prostitution movement to seventeen miles away to . . . Colombia. And I think that's going to be more evident in future days. . . . I just don't think this is a rape-murder case. . . . My gut is telling me that this is part of a transport, a prostitution business with the country of Colombia. I hear too many stories. I know too many people who have gone down to Aruba. . . . There are many instances where women go down there, that age, that type, blonde-haired, and they are drugged and transported to Colombia. . . ."

According to investigative journalist Tom Flocco, "bartenders from Cancun to Aruba to Jamaica regularly spike the drinks of unsuspecting women with so-called 'date-rape' drugs such as Rohypnol (roofies) and GHB (liquid Ecstasy), and reports describe the increasing use of these drugs to place women in a submissive state to move them into position for transport to Caribbean islands and South American brothels for indefinite periods for use as drugged prostitutes in known white sex slavery rings."

Further, the U.S. Department of State's *Trafficking in Person's Report* released by the Office to Monitor and Combat Trafficking in Persons, on June 3, 2005, states that ". . . the Netherlands Antilles and Aruba, autonomous regions within the Kingdom of the Netherlands, are transit and destination regions for trafficking of women and children for sexual exploitation." Additionally, it states, "In Curacao (and neighboring Aruba) observers estimate that 500 foreign women are in prostitution, some of whom may have been trafficked."

I do not know which is worse: knowing that Natalee may have been drugged, raped, and murdered, or wondering if she is alive and being held captive and forced into prostitution somewhere where I cannot get to her and save her. Those are some of the thoughts that haunt me each and every day. Not knowing anything is agonizing. So we have no choice but to keep moving forward with our search and continue to follow up on as many tips as we can.

The case seemed to be taking a positive turn when, on August 8, the police were considering questioning the Kalpoe brothers again. They said they would like to rearrest them, but they did not say on what grounds. At this time, we learned that Joran had recently turned eighteen and was going to be put into the prison's general population. Now, he would not be allowed to have daily visits from his father. Instead, he could only see him weekly and have three phone calls per month. We were hoping that he would finally break down and tell what he knew. Surely he knew more than he had revealed, but we were never really certain what, in fact, that was.

As I have already said, information regarding the progress of a criminal case is not as readily released in Aruba as it is in the United States, so we were not always clear on the status of the investigation. When the boys were all arrested, we had originally been told that no charges were ever brought against any of them and that, under Aruban law, charges are only made when someone goes to trial. Then, back in mid-July, Prosecutor Karin Janssen announced that all along the boys had been held on charges of "homicide and some other crimes which have a relationship with ending someone's life." When asked by reporters why she hadn't released that information earlier, she said, "In the first week of investigation, we wouldn't want to hurt the feelings of the family Holloway, because you couldn't speak about possible murder or homicide. Those people were finding a living daughter and we didn't find it suitable to talk about that."

According to the prosecutor, since Natalee had not been found, they felt it in poor taste to reveal their suspicions earlier. We knew there were differences between the way the United States handled criminal cases and the methods that Aruba used, but we did not know that things were being sugarcoated to protect us.

There was speculation that announcing the charges when Prosecutor Janssen did might have been a strategic move to put pressure on the suspects or to possibly appease us. She was being pressured herself from all sides to find a resolution. But, in the end, it appeared that the boys were actually being held on "suspicion" of rape and murder without any charges being brought against them, even though the prosecutor had publicly stated otherwise. Apparently, only a serious suspicion rather than solid evidence is necessary in Aruba to hold a suspect.

There certainly appeared to be enough suspicion to go around. A reporter came forward saying that he knew of witnesses who claimed that Joran approached Natalee two times at Carlos'n Charlie's on the night of her disappearance, and she rejected him. The second time, he supposedly hit her with a closed fist, and a friend from Mountain Brook intervened. If that was true, why didn't anyone come forward to keep him away from her? And it doesn't make sense that she would want to leave the bar with him after he hit her. Natalee would have never allowed herself to be treated so disrespectfully by a boy and then go with him, unless she didn't know what she was doing.

We were also informed that some of Natalee's hometown friends told Beth that when Natalee left the bar at the end of the evening, it was a mass exit with a flood of people running for cabs. It is important to note that all of the cabs in Aruba look different, and it is hard to tell which vehicle is a cab and which is not. They are not color-coded or specified by vehicle type as in the United States. Those that are identifiable only have a four-inch by eight-inch yellow plastic sign in the windshield and no other markings. They could be pick-up trucks, Honda Civics, station wagons, or whatever the family uses for a vehicle. Natalee's friend said that when Carlos'n Charlie's closed down, Natalee jumped into a car with the Kalpoe brothers thinking they were Aruban cab drivers.

We continued to hear conflicting stories as to the sequence of events leading up to Natalee's disappearance. One story was that Natalee told Joran that she wanted to go back to the Holiday Inn. He had previously told the group that he was on his school break from Holland and was staying at the same hotel. One detail that we are sure of is that Natalee never returned to her room at the Holiday Inn on her last night in Aruba. We were able to get a printout of the cards used to open her hotel room door on the night she disappeared. We know that it was opened three times after Natalee left the room. We have been able to account for all of the openings. Natalee's key was last used at 7:00 p.m. on Sunday evening May 29, 2005. All of the other keys were used early on May 30 and again prior to the kids leaving Aruba. Apparently, Natalee never returned to the room after she and her friends left to go out for the evening.

Joran had supposedly been introduced to Natalee while gambling in the casino the day before she disappeared. We were told that Natalee was not gambling, but rather observing her friend who was next to Joran and had lost almost $500. Joran helped the girl win back some of her money, so she called him her "lucky charm." Later, at Carlos'n Charlie's, Joran and Natalee supposedly walked out together. We were told that they were not holding hands or doing anything to indicate that they had become close. Another girl said she stopped Natalee and had a brief conversation with her. The girl indicated to us that Natalee appeared to be all right, but was not very talkative. The girl went off with her other friends. Supposedly Natalee then entered a vehicle in which Deepak was the driver. Deepak then called Satish to come out of the bar. He also entered the vehicle.

Another acquaintance of Natalee's from Mountain Brook High indicated that he remembered seeing the Kalpoe brothers and Joran at the Holiday Inn casino on Thursday, May 26, 2005. Natalee was there with the Mountain Brook students and the acquaintance saw her talking to the three boys. The students left to go to Carlos'n Charlie's, and later on they saw the three boys arrive there, and the acquaintance talked to them. They told him they were foreign exchange students studying in Aruba, and Joran said he was Dutch. The boy's opinion of Joran was that he was "quiet and non-assuming," and that "many of the Mountain Brook girls, including Natalee, thought he was hot." He described Deepak as a "short, obnoxious guy who kept getting in his face" to the point where he had to shove him away. Deepak shoved him back, and another Mountain Brook student broke them up.

The next night, many of the Mountain Brook students gathered at Carlos'n Charlie's. The three boys were also there. The acquaintance hung out with the other Mountain Brook students, including Natalee, and they were all drinking a lot. He said that Natalee appeared to be attracted to Joran, but it was Deepak who showed an interest in Natalee. Everyone was dancing during the night and, at one point, Natalee got up on the bar and danced. The acquaintance followed, then others joined them. When the bar was closing, the acquaintance went out front to catch a cab with some people he had met from another high school. He said that he noticed that he and Natalee were the last two Mountain Brook students to leave the bar. He had been outside with his three new friends when he saw Natalee exit the bar by herself.

She told him that she was looking for someone. He knew from hanging out with her in the bar that she had been drinking, but she was walking without assistance and talking coherently. He offered to have her join him and his friends for the cab ride back to the hotel, but she said no. Instead, she reentered the bar. After about fifteen or twenty minutes, the boy again saw Natalee emerge from Carlos'n Charlie's, but now she was stumbling and needed Deepak's assistance to walk. They walked away, and the acquaintance never saw her again.

I spoke to a police investigator on one of my trips back to Aruba over the months following Natalee's disappearance, and he told me that, based on the way her acquaintance described her, the drug GHB was probably administered to her. If someone is affected by GHB, the people they are with gain complete control over them. Taking the drug is like flipping a light switch. The person who slips the girl the drug has the control. Then the next day, the girl has no recollection of the events.

The mother of the acquaintance indicated that the FBI had not taken the boy's statement seriously. I was subsequently told that the Aruban police were never informed of his statement. We have heard that the boy feels terrible about not having taken any action now that Natalee is missing. There was no way that he could have known what would happen next. They had all been out taking Jell-O shots from what we were told, something they cannot freely or legally do at home due to their ages. They probably indulged more than they should have during this time of celebration, and they were not thinking clearly. Whatever happened to Natalee that night can only be blamed on the person or persons who took advantage of her and those who may have aided them and not on any other individual. Her friends need to know that we do not harbor any ill will toward any one of them.

Some other witnesses, possibly Mountain Brook kids, said they saw Natalee in a vehicle with Joran, Deepak, and Satish as it circled the bar to leave. Natalee was in the back with Joran while Deepak was driving and Satish was in the front passenger seat. The kids yelled for the vehicle to stop, but it kept going. Nobody realized the seriousness of the situation. How could they? These were innocent, fun-loving kids who were commemorating their graduation together. They had no idea what kind of danger Natalee was in or that they wouldn't all just meet up the next day for their trip home as planned. However, later on, apparently some of her friends did become concerned about her failure to return to the Holiday Inn, and they waited in the hotel lobby until 5 a.m. for her to return.

Leads continued to pour in, and we tried to follow up on each one. Art Wood, who had been continuously searching the island, found a belt on the beach near the lighthouse. It was a significant find because it looked exactly like one that Joran had used on his Web site to simulate choking one of his friends. Looking at the picture made me cringe. Joran had a smile on his face while his "victim" looked like he was in pain. If Joran thought strangling someone was funny, I was afraid to imagine what he might have done to Natalee. In the end, the police decided the belt was too old and weathered to be part of the case, so it was not tested for DNA. Since the belt in the photo on Joran's Web site also looked old, it did not make sense to me to disregard its significance as evidence. But nothing was making any sense in the investigation, so they were being consistent with either their ineptness or their apparent cover-up.

Art gave the belt to detectives and then arranged to have Fred Golba, a professional searcher, scour the area. On August 12, 2005, the search-and-rescue dog teams that were specially trained to search for bodies came in to hunt for clues. They got all excited in the area where the belt was found. Fred excavated the area further and found two small, milky pieces of plastic. He wanted to have them sent for forensics testing, but Dennis Jacobs, the lead investigator who was present for the finding of the plastic and saw how upset the dogs had gotten, considered them to be irrelevant and told Fred to throw them away. So, again, a potential piece of evidence was ignored.

Then a private investigator found a man who said he helped someone bury a woman's body with a few other men the night Natalee disappeared. He was put into a psychiatric institution, but the private detective talked to him and some others and his statements were consistent with the witness who said he saw someone bury a woman's body in the landfill three days after Natalee vanished.

Another witness, a jogger who said he lived close to the Marriott Hotel and wanted to remain anonymous, had called authorities early in the investigation saying he saw the three boys on the night that Natalee disappeared digging around the same area where the gardener had seen them. He was asked through the media to come forward again because the police finally considered his information valuable. Slowly more evidence was coming to light. We heard more about the cage that was stolen from the fishermen huts. On the night after Natalee disappeared, three out of four fishermen's huts on the beach near where she and Joran allegedly went were burglarized. Missing from one of the huts was a knife and a cage used to trap fish. Supposedly the fisherman forgot until much later to report the incident. He finally called it in but was not contacted back. Apparently the cage was made of wire and had an opening at one end where the fish enter and cannot get back out. It was usually weighted and baited and put in the water with a buoy to mark its location. It was big enough to hold a human body, and the theory is that Natalee was put in there and taken out to sea. In an e-mail I had received, someone discussing the cages stated that "a lock was broken, and the net was used to dump Natalee two miles off-shore." I asked the police to check all this out, and, on a later trip to Aruba, I met with a detective who was assigned to stay near the Marriott Hotel from 11:00 p.m. to 6:00 a.m. to determine the tourist activity around the fishermen's huts. He said there were too many people there for any activity to occur. He felt that if the boys had been there with Natalee, there would have been witnesses. He didn't think it was likely they ever went to the beach.

In late August, something significant happened. Art Wood released information that a sixteen-year-old Aruban girl was preparing to go to the police to file a complaint stating that she had been drugged and date-raped by Joran only a few weeks before Natalee's disappearance. She also claimed that he had done the same thing to two of her friends. She was afraid to tell her parents, but she did tell an attorney who then reported the incident to a child advocate who was from the Aruban authorities. She supposedly told her story to the police after that.

Shortly after the information about the girl came out, women from other countries were also reported to be coming forward with similar allegations. It might not have necessarily helped in Natalee's case, but it could have helped to keep him in custody while the investigation continued.

It was difficult to hear about so many leads that appeared to be significant enough to keep Joran in jail, when, in fact, they weren't really making any difference in the case at all. But I continued to follow up on as many as I could in order to rule out all possibilities in my own investigation.

Natalee had been missing for over two and a half months, and I still hadn't reached the point where I could shake off the feeling that this was just a nightmare that was happening to someone else. I used to see things like this, a story on the news, a tragedy in a foreign country that we watched in horror, but I had never considered the possibility that we could be personally affected by any of it. Unfortunately, I was wrong.

FIVE

HelpfindNatalee@comcast.net

THE LACK OF ANY HARD EVIDENCE INDICATING WHAT happened to Natalee was ripping my heart out. I needed to find my daughter. Any clues were like gold to the investigation. There was absolutely nothing solid to go on which sometimes led me to believe that either the entire island was enjoying watching us suffer, or a stronger force, such as corrupt officials, or some high-level outside entity like the Mafia, would not allow anyone to speak up. Were people afraid to talk out of fear of retaliation? I had to find an answer, and it appeared that no one was willing to come forward. It was apparent that sifting through all of the materials that I had put together during my own investigation was not going to bring Natalee home. I had to find something else. I struggled to figure out where to look next. There had to be something I was missing. Then it came to me. What if there was a way that people could contact me while remaining anonymous? Maybe someone would feel free to say what he or she knew if they were sure their identities would not be revealed.

As I sat in front of my computer and opened another e-mail from a good-hearted soul who wanted to become part of the case, I realized that the answer was right in front of my face: "You've Got Mail." I saw that I had an e-mail from a detective who had written to me before. He was someone who I may have previously assumed was only looking for fame and fortune by being connected with my publicity. He wrote to me in the hopes that I would bring him into the action. I read through his e-mail carefully, and since he did not offer anything of substance, I deleted it, but not before an idea was born. What if I was able to solve the crime through the Internet? If someone could come forward and give me anything, a lead, a name, a simple clue to save my Natalee or help nail her assailants, then I could give the information to the prosecutor's office, and the informant would remain anonymous and safe. That was it! I would use the Internet and reach the masses without anyone fearing intimidation.

With the help of my sister, Linda, and the rest of my family, I set up e-mail addresses where people could send messages to me about the case. The response was unbelievable. We had so many e-mails that we had to set up another, and another, such as:

HelpfindNatalee@comcast.net

Hope_for_Natalee@yahoo.com

Investigation_for_Natalee@yahoo.com

Soon, we were up and running. The biggest problem we faced was how we would differentiate between a real lead and supposition, but we decided we would just have to figure that out as we went along. My wife, Robin, and I started reading through the massive e-mails. My sister, Linda, did the same. I even had my father-in-law, Melvin Parten, and others pouring through each and every one of them.

They began coming immediately. There were many different types of e-mails arriving. Some had what appeared to be serious clues. Others were from people who sent their best wishes. Then there were those filled with hyperbole. There were also some incredibly long and detailed e-mails. One such letter included information that, at first glance, appeared to be worth checking out, until I realized that it was from someone merely trying to endear himself to us. I ended my contact with him. Someone else sent an e-mail claiming that Natalee was not in Aruba, but was being held in an apartment in California. I handed over the lead to the Birmingham FBI office but never heard anything about it again. The following e-mails are examples of what we have had to wade through. They were added here unedited except for length; spelling and grammatical errors have been left intact. However, we have eliminated any features that would allow identification of or contact with an author.

Subject: Natalee
Date: June 25, 2005
From: Infoperson
To: helpfindnatalee@comcast.net

During a poignant, tearful, emotional interview between Greta and Beth, as we were eating at the dinner table, our psychic and clairvoyant eight year old son, with his back to the television, went into one of his staring-interdimensional/trance-like states, stating with emphasis, extemporaneously: "They put her in the lighthouse until she dies, they locked her in there until she was dead. They did something bad to her and hid her. Somebody (with emphasis) 'who knew what they were doing' (less emphasis) locked her in the lighthouse. Then they buried it so noone would find it . . . in the dirt somewhere. The two boys who were in jail know. The two Mexican boys didn't do it, the other two did it." This, in part, was reported orally via phone to FBI hotline in AL a couple of weeks ago the day that the reward was announced. Sincerely, we tried to get this on tape to you, but the ole southern boy FBI agent said he wouldn't tape it. We wish no reward and complete anonymity. May God be guiding you in your search for your precious one.

I know the person meant well, but I guess they do not realize what their story looks like to someone who is not a "believer." The next e-mail came in from a person who said they have a film that is related to Natalee's case.

Subject: Natalee
Date: June 29, 2005
From: helpinguInfoperson
To: helpfindnatalee@comcast.net

Dave—Important—A Film Found Online Related To Natalee's Case

Dave—you and the FBI need to see this film—who ever filmed it knew too much about Natalee's case to be accidental—may definitely be related to the case! A week or two after she was missing, this was filmed—way before some of these locations were known, the pond area, rocky beach like where the park ranger was, and refinery, etc.

The FBI can probably track down the site and get their home address—and maybe grab the tape. Who knows what else was taped and may still be at their house . . . Read all the way down . . . Today there is a different message than yesterday—but sure does seem related to the case.

The posts:

Now there is a message to extradite Joran. I wonder if these boys were part of the "pimp" gang—maybe even Freddie that was arrested today? He was reported to be the cameraman of the group.

Found some strange videos of Aruba. Not sure what they are, but gives some insight on the terrain in Aruba. It had a video that was showing searching between some rocks near a beach. I think it was probably a week or two after she was missing. I saved the video, but never really looked at it again. But when I watched it again, I noticed that the video had a "watermark" of the website name over the picture and it was the aru-bay.com site. So I went back there to see if there were more videos. In the one video, the person gets out of the car near a retention pond (not sure if it was the one that was drained) and for a split second, you can see that the person holding the video camera is barefoot and they have dark skin. I'm glad you found it too because I never got any feedback when I posted it earlier. It is just strange and I wondered the same thing . . . are they traveling around filming areas connected to the case. That page is VERY weird . . . . . it should be sent to greta! or the FBI!!!

I just watched the clip "To Be Continued" it is a video of a party on the Tattoo. Some scary people made this, no doubt about it. A girl with Natalee's face is dancing, and another, in a conga line, wears a sequined top like the one Natalee wore when she danced with her squad on the football field. The perspective is that of a predator, and the sense is that this is a familiar routine.

At the end, the camera pans on a location near the refinery. It is a frightening thing. Implies a 4th and a 5th suspect, #4 selecting Natalee out of the crowd on Tattoo by way of #5's video-feed. Sure gives "we left her at the beach" bit more bite. So, then. The question is this: would the mysterious #4 be dumb enough to publish something approaching the truth on the internet? Might she have met up with an ego that big? I don't know, but somebody went to some effort to suggest so. Scary.

Yes—and then "Sequel" after it. I got the distinct impression it was a 'message' being sent. Vague, but a message. Both were filmed on the "Tattoo" and both prominently featured blondes doing suggestive dancing.

Not sure why I got the ominous vibe from it, depicting his next victim dancing at an outdoor concert. now a message on their front page stating

"The Digital Dub Deciples are now signing off" and they removed the links to all of their videos! Good thing I saved them all before they shut it down.

There were other e-mails from those offering theories, such as the following:

Subject: Natalee
Date: July 1, 2005
From: theoryhelpInfoperson
To: helpfindnatalee@comcast.net

THEORY . . . . NATALEE is alive, was kidnapped, and she is being hidden somewhere, as yet not found, on ARUBA or elsewhere (on 6-29 BETH was on "CNN" and said that she was SURE that the 3 boys in custody had something to do with NATALEE's "kidnapping")

THEORY . . . . NATALEE died after self-induced alcohol overdose consumption and/or self-induced or surreptitiously induced drug(s) overdose and/or while swimming, etc. and her body is in the ocean or somewhere, as yet not found, on ARUBA or elsewhere

THEORY . . . . NATALEE died after self-induced alcohol overdose consumption and/or self-induced or surreptitiously induced drug(s) overdose and/or while swimming, etc. while with Main Suspect J. SLOOT and/or some other person(s) who encountered her after 1:50 AM, then Main Suspect J. SLOOT and/or some other person(s) she was with "freaked-out" and alone decided (or was aided by other person(s) after-the-fact) to dispose of her body in the ocean, or hidden somewhere, as yet not found, on ARUBA or elsewhere

THEORY . . . . NATALEE died while with Main Suspect J. SLOOT and/or some other person(s), possibly in conjunction with earlier—known or unknown to NATALEE introduced chemical drugs— then Main Suspect J. SLOOT and/or some other person(s) he contacted decided (or was aided by other person(s) after-the-fact) to dispose of her body in the ocean, or hidden somewhere, as yet not found, on ARUBA or elsewhere.

It is tedious for the parent of a missing child to read through thousands of messages like these in the hopes that at least one person might have a real lead. As I have mentioned before, it is like looking for the needle without knowing where the haystack is. E-mails also arrived reporting on various rumors that were going around. I considered them to be in the same category as the theories:

Subject: Natalee
Date: July 4, 2005
From: rumormongerInfoperson
To: helpfindnatalee@comcast.net

RUMOR . . . . Somewhere on the island are abandoned mineshafts (possibly the "Bushiribana Gold Mill Ruins") that are very deep (one estimated at 800')

RUMOR . . . . sharks are daily/regularly fed heavily by ARUBANs on the east side of island in an attempt (apparently successful, if it is, in fact, done regularly) to try and keep sharks concentrated there, far away from the north, south, and west beaches where the hotels and tourists mostly are.

RUMOR . . . . Somewhere on the island is a large fire incinerator. (a mortuary(s) would also probably have one, possibly even an animal veterinarian(s))

RUMOR . . . . There are rumors that several different witnesses claim they saw the two Current Suspect KALPOE's cleaning the "Honda" car at a spot away from their home after NATALEE disappeared.

Sometimes, an inkling of a rumor would make sense, and we would pay more attention to it. I never completely discounted anything. I always tried to investigate as many as leads as possible. So we considered the following hypothesis:

Subject: Natalee
Date: June 9, 2005
From: hypothesisInfoperson
To: helpfindnatalee@comcast.net

HYPOTHESIS . . . . by 2:00-2:35 NATALEE was alive (possibly unconscious), or dead.

IF she was alive when Main Suspect J. SLOOT, supposedly, left her alone on the beach, she may have "run away" deliberately, been kidnapped, died accidentally, committed suicide, or was murdered before 2:30 by Main Suspect J. SLOOT or after 2:30 by a person(s) who

encountered her somewhere after Main Suspect J. SLOOT, supposedly, left her alone on the beach (Main Suspect J. SLOOT claims she
told him she wanted to say at the beach)

It appeared that people were staying awake all night long analyzing every little fact they saw on Fox News and MSNBC. It
amazed me how some individuals would lose the semblance of
their own life and become completely entrenched in my daughter's
disappearance. Mind you, I am grateful for all of the caring people
who have tried to help, but it was clear that some of them did not
realize when something was a valid lead and when what they said
was nothing more than speculation and guessing. What we so desperately needed was a real tip, one that would lead us to Natalee,
or at the very least, to the truth about what happened to her.

Occasionally we received messages that, while they did not
contain any valuable information, made us feel grateful for the
supportive and kind words, like the next two e-mails:

Subject: Natalee
Date: June 15, 2005
From: likestohelpInfoperson
To: helpfindnatalee@comcast.net

in some way, i don't have any info, i don't know natalee or the family i
just want to see justice done for her.. i guess thats like many americans, i just want to know is there something i can do? who can i
write(written bama's gov, the dutch), i've donated $$, i want to help in
some way. natalee reminds me of girls ive dated, she reminds me of
my nieces and i know that, god forbid if anything happened to them i'd
want people helping me. if there is anything i can do, let me know. i'm
just one american who will never forget natalee, and would like to help.

Subject: Natalee
Date: June 18, 2005
From: help4uInfoperson
To: helpfindnatalee@comcast.net

Hello again,

Your plight has not been forgotten.

Initially, I was opposed to the boycott of tourism in Aruba, but after all that has happened, it seems pretty clear the reason the case of Natalee's disappearance wasn't resolved is political. At this point, to make any progress, you're going to have to target their pocketbook. I hope that Nancy Grace, Catherine Crier and others are back in touch with you soon and could help spearhead this for you.

Just know there are many of us who still think of Natalee every day and want so much for those responsible to be brought to justice.

Some of the messages appeared to be possible leads until we read them in total.

Subject: Natalee
Date: June 21, 2005
From: inadreamInfoperson
To: helpfindnatalee@comcast.net

Dear Dave,

I don't make up stories.; I'm not looking to collect reward money, nor do I want any publicity. Your daughter, Natalee, appeared to me, on Sunday night, July 10, and showed me where Joran dumped her body. Before I get to that, I saw, in person, that Natalee has 2 dimples above the corners of her mouth; the right one only shows up when she laughs. I raved about them to my family for almost 2 full weeks before cable news started airing photos which proved my claim. Also, I heard her voice when she spoke to give me a message for her mom- Natalee's voice is deeper than Beth's, and she has hardly any accent. When the news stations first ran that now famous home video of her in the car, they ran the footage without any introduction- I recognized Natalee's voice from the other end of my house and came running to see her. I realize that these are subjective proofs, but my family can verify that I spoke frequently of them before they were subsequently proven true by news broadcasts. Please pour as much manpower as humanly possible into following up on my information- Natalee gave it to me herself and I know it is legitimate.

On Sunday night, July 10,2005, I had just gone to bed when she suddenly appeared before me, looking beautiful and happy. I was so surprised, I said, "Natalee! How ARE you?" She flashed me a big laughing smile (at which point I saw both of those dimples), and said, "Good! then asked her where Joran had disposed of her body. Abruptly, she disappeared and a nighttime scene unfolded before my eyes:

I was looking at a large dirt field, in which Joran was holding Natalee under the arms, like in a bear hug. Her body was limp and her head was flopped to one side; long blonde hair was hanging everywhere. Joran slowly lowered her into some kind of cylindrical tube that came up from the ground, about 2 1/2- 3 feet, It was barely larger in diameter than her body. As I watched, it reminded me of that incident that occurred about 15 years ago in Texas, when baby Jessica fell down into that well. I said to Natalee, "A well?" and she replied, "Not a well, a CISTERN!"

That was the end of the vision, but it is burned into my memory. The field was rectangular, fairly large, and had foliage along the left border- shrubs and maybe some trees, but not heavily wooded. They seemed to be about 10—15 feet high, possibly planted as a windbreak for the crops. The earth had been turned, as in a plowed field, and there was cut STRAW scattered across the entire area. It must have been a grain crop that had been harvested. Also, there were at least 2 or 3 more of these same "cisterns" placed around the field.

At the time of this vision, I did not know what a cistern was; I had to look it up in the dictionary. As I later discovered, cisterns are widely used on Aruba for water storage. Also, Aruba apparently has no irrigation, so it seems plausible that farmers would have multiple cisterns in a crop field to facilitate the watering of the crops.

If the grain crop had recently been harvested at the end of May, that field would look completely different now if a new crop had since been planted.

My research indicates that only 10% of the island (12 sq. miles) is arable land, so a crop field should be relatively easy to locate.

I am so sorry you have had to endure this horrible tragedy, but please know that Natalee is doing great now. While it is a terrible tragedy to your family, Natalee is not tormented or suffering at all. There is always a Divine plan at work. I understand she wanted to be a pediatrician and help children; she has done so much more good on behalf of children world-wide than anyone could have ever dreamed. She is truly a wonderful girl and she will always be with you. She has become everyone's daughter.

You and Beth have been an inspiration to the world (and the rest of your families, as well). Best of luck in your search, and I hope my info leads you to Natalee soon.

We received many e-mails from psychics. There are more "psychics" out there than I ever imagined. Astrologers offered to help as well. I have received so many e-mails from them that it is a wonder that every crime in the world has not been solved by now. For that matter, with all of these people who claim to "know" things, I would think they could actually prevent some of the horrible events that have occurred. However, none of them have been able to lead us to Natalee. So, I am doubtful about their true abilities.

One person claiming to be a psychic wanted to meet me in Aruba and offered to pay for his own trip. He contacted me two times saying that he was from Europe and that he would show me where Natalee is. He was insistent upon meeting me in person. I didn't take him up on his offer. If he had real information, why couldn't he just give me the facts over the phone? Maybe he was really looking for a photo op with me for his Web site. I'll never know what true motives some of these people had. For now, he is just another person waiting in line with hundreds of other psychics.

An e-mail came in from a woman who is a close friend of a psychic who claimed to find people who are missing with a 99 percent accuracy rate. She said that there is a huge cover-up by Paulus van der Sloot and that anyone bringing forth information is afraid they will be killed or harmed because he has a lot of clout. To be honest, I did not think we needed a psychic to give us doubts about Paulus, but I respect the woman for trying to help.

The e-mails and calls kept coming in, and they got stranger and more detailed as the days passed. Someone sent one insisting he knew Natalee's whereabouts. He said he had it from "a respectable source that she was abducted in Aruba against her will by a Mafia-like group" and brought to "Colombia, then flown to Siskiyou, County, Ca." She was supposedly being "held captive inside a room in a house along del Monte St., Montague City, Siskiyou, County, Ca." A satellite map with a yellow arrow pointing to the house was included with the e-mail. He suggested that we keep the information a secret and "let the FBI check it out." He considered the "group behind this" to be "highly organized and well connected." Oh, and he added that he has been "motivated by the reward for her safe return by her family."

While reading through the e-mails, I was sent some links to blogs about Natalee. That's where I saw the spin from Aruba. The boys and their supporters were going to use the Internet to fight us for speaking out against them. Some of the people on the blogs were defending the boys:

> I am in Joran Van der Sloot's corner because I believe he is being treated in a way that makes Lady Justice not only cover her eyes but shed tears from them. There is NO HARD EVIDENCE against Joran and 9/10 of what we call evidence will splatter if it hits the barn floor. As long as we have a steady diet of guess and speculation I will stay on the side that treats Joran fair. Friend of Joran

I cannot agree with him. I think the evidence is definitely in our favor. If the fact that Joran told numerous versions of his night with Natalee is not a clear indication that he has something to hide about what happened, then call me paranoid! There were a couple of more postings in favor of the boys:

> I doubt any of three guys committed any crime they are accused of.
> 1. I think someone else . . . either a friend she made while in aruba picked her up after the boys dropped her.
> 2. A stranger who took advantage of her and shipped her else where.
> 3. She planned to escape the life she was having back home and moved forward with someones help.

> All the media, speculation etc is probably making it difficult for her to turn the clock back but if she is out there she should return after all there are three guys whose lives and future have been badly damaged.

Another possibility is that maybe Joran knows who she went along with after he dropped her and he probably is unable to talk because he is protecting himself and his family from any harm. Thats my opinion.

And another:

I think Joran is innocent and I pray to God that he can go home to his family tomorrow I think Natalee did not want to go to the University of AL I think that is what her mother wanted her to do so she could brag. Natalee probably never had any choices with a mother like Beth all the footage of Natalee dancing what is that for anyway except for Beth to brag. I think Natalee had someone help her leave the island. She did write the Quote in her Year book form Free bird I feel so sad for the Van Der Sloot family and I do pray for God to help them through this.

Others were sure of Joran's guilt:

what makes you think that Joran is not the one. Usually when you have hooked up with a girl you make sure you take her home and kiss her goodnight. Why did Joran lie to begin with. Why was story made up before her mother got there. What are you living under a rock. Have you not read what's been going on in the case. What the hell do mean when does a boy become responsible for a girl? What are you friend of Joran's. Boys usually don't lie if they know they have nothing to with it. Wake up.

And another:

The absurdity of the jvds left her at the beach and then something happened to her theory is that jdvs is implicating himself with his own alibi. The odds of harm coming to a girl left alone in the middle of the night in an isolated place with no one knowing about it are very small when you consider the odds she will just sleep until daylight, the odds of running into a criminal as opposed to someone who would help her, the odds that a criminal would be deterred by the risk of punishment if he were caught, and the odds that she could evade an attacker, scare him off by screaming, or summon help from someone else in the event of an attack. If she were left alone and then harmed, the over-whelming odds are that the harm was inflicted by someone one told by one or more of the suspects that she was there or by someone who was it cahoots with the suspects from the beginning and knew where the suspects were taking her. You would have to be a ninny like Anita to think otherwise.

One more:

Aruba disinformation wants us to believe that crime against tourists is almost non-existant but yet they also want us to believe Natalee would have the bad luck to not only run into one possible kidnapper/rapist/ murderer but two or more in one night. possible-ok at this point maybe, but the odds? very unlikely. too many other more plausible explanations just as you pointed out. they need to re-search every square inch of his apartment—and what about the condo at the racquet club—is there really one & has it been searched? i too feel there is another location involved—especially if this was a planned routine for them—they would have some place more private than a public beach.

This one really got to me. Someone actually wrote, "If Natalee was black, it would never have been televised." That was hurtful. I had never thought about anything like that before. I had never thought about any of this. Most people are not aware of what this type of situation is like until it happens to them. If what they said was true, I am very disturbed by that. But I cannot take my daughter's story out of the news until I feel that we have all of the answers that we need. I hope that all missing persons would be treated with an equal amount of concern. But I do not believe that the issue lies within my power to change, especially right now. I am a parent in distress. I am barely able to help myself. I need all of the support I can get.

Some people on the blogs offered helpful messages like the following one: "Natalee's family has posted a reward of $1,000,000 for Natalee's safe return, along with $250,000 for a tip to Natalee's whereabouts, for a life-changing total of $1,250,000, no questions asked." They then listed four of our e-mail addresses to forward tips.

We received an e-mail from a "tracker" who wrote with information about where to find Natalee.

Subject: concerning your daughter's whereabouts
Date: June 25, 2005
From: trackherforuInfoperson
To: helpfindnatalee@comcast.net

Dear Mr. Holloway

I am a professional bail bonds man and tracker, but most importantly I'm the father of six children. My heart goes out to you and that's why I am submitting this e-mail in hopes of recovering your daughter Natalee or any physical evidence which would close the Sept. 4 window for those seeking freedom. These people that you are dealing with are slicker than you think. I have condensed and made tracking info as simple as possible, including a crude map. The map will be an attachment, it is safe to open. Continually have a presence on the southern most third of Arashi beach-this I believe will make people extremely nervous. Expect diversions while there-sightings/other things found across the island. These are intended to move the search away. Someone may just crack as long as you are there.

In my opinion, Natalee (or parts of her) is buried on the southern most third of Arashi Beach adjacent to Boca Catalina. I believe she is located either at the lower half of the distance between low-mean water and high tide; at the base of a seaward facing dune;1-10ft. seaward from a flora run(brush/groundcover/trees) all of which is directly centered in a line with each Boca in that area particularly within an arch/horseshoe pattern consisting of natural elements or scattered within the honeycombed rock near or in a boca with the arch pattern. Her grave is most likely marked with singular or multiple natural objects either standing alone or in a pattern.

If the areas have been searched as shown in map do not give up. Follow these instructions. I believe Natalee is buried in plain sight.

My stomach turned when I read, "In my opinion, Natalee (or parts of her) is buried on the southern most third of Arashi Beach . . ." I realize that he was trying to help, but there is a way to do that with a small amount of sensitivity, isn't there?

One of the most interesting e-mails follows. Imagine every husband, wife, and child in the world being implanted with "The Human Lo Jack System":

Subject: Abduction to South America
Date: July 5, 2005
From: lojackInfoperson
To: helpfindnatalee@comcast.net

I strongly suspect that Natalee was sold to Venezuelan sex slavers. The numerous false reports and lies are merely a smoke screen to divert attention from this possibility.

What should have been done, as I wrote on several web sites, was to avoid publicizing the reward in South America. Instead, send the reward notices to the police departments in SA. Regardless of their connections with the brothels, for that kind of money, those cops would sell their own mothers. Had this been done, every brothel in the country would have been raided, and hopefully Beth would have received a tearful, joyous phone call. If Natalee is never found, I suggest that the reward money be used to prevent such disappearances in the future. . . . The money could be used to form a company to solve the disappearance problem.

A human "Lo Jack" system could be developed. Every child, every young woman, in fact all people, could carry hidden on their person, an RF device the person can trigger to notify the police they are in trouble, and give their GPS location. It could also act as a transponder, so that when the person is missing, loved ones or police could activate it to find the victim. Such devices are used to track wild animals. Why not humans?

That suggestion is a bit too much like George Orwell's classic *1984* where he describes a world in which Big Brother is watching us. So, I moved on to the next e-mail.

I never know what information awaits me when I open the e-mails. But I promise this, until I have a resolution, I will read every single one of them. Anything that has a semblance of credibility will be thoroughly investigated.

SIX

Web of Deceit

THE DUTCH SYSTEM OF JUSTICE HAS TAUGHT US A HARD lesson, and we learned it at the expense of our daughter, Natalee. We are used to living in a country where people reach out to help when you are in trouble, when there's a death, a job loss, an illness, or a crime. I can say with complete honesty that the Aruban population, in general, came out in droves to help with our search and was supportive about our situation.

However, there appears to be a major difference between Aruba and the United States when it comes to the way the authorities handle criminal investigations. Here in the United States, police and prosecutors go to great lengths in their search for the truth. They do everything they can to prosecute guilty parties. When evidence is presented that clearly demonstrates a person's involvement in a crime, there is no question that a thorough investigation will take place, at which time, depending upon the type of crime committed, the suspect's possessions will be seized, DNA analysis will be performed, fingerprints will be looked for and tested, blood stains will be analyzed, witnesses will give statements, and any other relevant information will become part of the prosecutor's case. Everything is taken seriously, even circumstantial evidence.

It is hard to cover up a crime in the United States. We hear all the time about the misdeeds of well-known people, including political figures, government officials, police officers, and people in the entertainment industry. Even a president has been taken down for his misconduct. That is not to say that some people are not able to get around the law. But, for the most part, justice applies equally here when a crime is committed. Prosecutors make it a point to keep the victims and families updated on the progress of their investigation and even take into consideration the families' wishes when recommending the consequences that a defendant will face.

So it came as a great disappointment to us when we were first introduced to the Aruban/Dutch system of justice, where government officials—people in charge of the welfare of their citizens— could take such apparently credible evidence as in Natalee's case and openly and blatantly shove it aside as if it had no bearing on her disappearance. But that, in and of itself, was not the worst of it. As time passed, we slowly witnessed what we believed to be an incredible and continuing pattern of lies and strange activity that was occurring behind the scenes. Once we took the time to fit all of the following pieces together, the picture was not so much about who is responsible for Natalee's disappearance, but rather, who is in charge of the apparent ongoing and ever-expanding conspiracy to keep the truth about it from surfacing.

Aruba has a reputation for being a tourist-friendly paradise. I think by now the world is aware that bad things happen there, and if the responsible party is well-connected, nobody is held accountable. What people do not know is just how deeply ingrained the cover-up on that island actually is. The fact that Paulus van der Sloot was a justice official at one time and that his son may have gotten away with a serious crime is just the beginning.

It was clear from my very first phone call to the Aruban police that something was not right. My daughter was missing, and the detective was too busy to get on the phone with me. When we first arrived in Aruba, barely anyone, including the police, were aware of Natalee's disappearance. Even though we had explained that she had been there on her high-school graduation trip, that she was due to arrive home the previous day, and that there had been no word from her, they told us that she must be out having fun. When all of her belongings were found sitting in her hotel room, including her passport, and her friends told stories about how she looked like she was lost and how she had gotten into a car with three boys who refused to stop when they were called out to, there was still no concern.

The three boys, Joran van der Sloot and Deepak and Satish Kalpoe, admitted being with Natalee, and admitted to a number of different and changing stories about her last night on the island. The list seems endless, starting with their first account, that they dropped her off at her hotel and that she stumbled out of the car and tripped. When Joran attempted to help her up, Natalee supposedly told him that she could stand on her own. As she walked away, the boys saw the security guards coming toward her to help, so they drove away.

In another version of the story, Deepak supposedly told his mother that he and his brother, Satish, were driving Natalee and Joran to the hotel. He said that he did not like it that Natalee and Joran were kissing in the back seat of his car, so he told them to go get a room somewhere. But on the way back to the hotel, Natalee asked if they would drive her to see the California Lighthouse, because it was her last night there and she hadn't seen it yet. Deepak said he drove her up there, but she was so drunk, he never stopped the car.

After that, the story changed once again. Satish told his mother that the reason they lied was because they were covering for their friend, Joran, who had snuck out of the house that night. He also told her that he and Deepak left Joran and Natalee at the beach by the Marriott Hotel and went home. However, we heard that while the authorities were questioning all three boys, Joran claimed that Deepak and Satish took him home while Natalee was still in the car with them. He supposedly added that he and Natalee exchanged e-mail addresses and he left. He said that Deepak and Satish then drove Natalee back to the Holiday Inn. Deepak adamantly denied Joran's version and asked Joran why he was lying.

The next story also came from Joran. This time he told his mother that he and the Kalpoe brothers took Natalee to the lighthouse, then they went to the Marriott Hotel beach where he and Natalee got out of the car and stayed there by themselves. He said they kissed and fooled around, then she supposedly told him that she wanted to stay at the beach alone, so he left her there. He promised he did not do anything to hurt her.

Now, fast forward and Joran is in prison. He supposedly begins to cry and confesses that "we buried Natalee" by the fishermen's huts near the Marriott Hotel. Subsequently, police escorted Joran, Deepak, and Satish one at a time to the beach by the Marriott Hotel and also to the fishermen's huts where Joran claimed that they buried Natalee. The police wanted to see whether the boys' stories matched. Nothing was found to suggest that Natalee had even been there.

But then Joran changed his story back to leaving Natalee alone at the beach, saying that she had fallen asleep. He now allegedly claimed that he believed that Deepak found her, raped and murdered her, then buried her near the fishermen's huts, according to a report from FBI profiler Clint van Zandt.

He later changed that version a little by saying that he and Natalee both fell asleep and that he woke up and left her there. But he continued to maintain that Deepak returned and killed Natalee and buried her.

After telling all of those differing versions of events regarding the night they were with Natalee, still nobody took the situation seriously. The boys were questioned and released, giving them plenty of time to wash their car and dispose of evidence, possibly even a body.

It did not even seem strange to Aruban and Dutch officials that one of the boys, Joran, had free reign in such places as bars and casinos. After all, he was only seventeen years old: too young to legally even enter those places. Then we found out that, not only did he frequent them, he was apparently so well-known in the bars and casinos that he was allowed to run tabs. He gambled alongside his father, a man who had been in effect dethroned from his soon-to-be position of authority as a judge due to his alleged ineptness, a man whose own explanation of the night Natalee disappeared could not even be trusted, and finally, a man who, by his own admission, would do anything he could to protect his son.

The fact that Joran snuck out of his house, that he lied to his parents, that he allegedly admitted having sex with Natalee while she went in and out of consciousness, but then denied ever touching her—this did not raise suspicion. The fact that his father covered for him, first claiming to have picked Joran up at McDonald's at 4:00 a.m. on May 30, then, changing the time to 11:00 p.m. on May 29, hours before a witness saw Joran with the Kalpoe brothers where they claimed they had dropped Natalee off much earlier—this did not create a stir.

Much later, we heard another version of events about that

night. The Kalpoe brothers claimed that they dropped Joran and Natalee off at the beach sometime around 1:30 a.m. and that Joran had called them around 2:40 a.m. to say that he was alone, that he had left Natalee on the beach, and that he needed a ride. However, a lawyer for one of the Kalpoe brothers said that Joran had called the boys to tell them that he was alone, that he left Natalee at the beach, and that he was walking home. The brothers claimed to have been home at the time. Supposedly, records show that Deepak had been on the Internet between 2:00 a.m. and 3:00 a.m. Of course, there is no way to verify that it was actually Deepak. Someone else could have been using his account. Another possibility is that Deepak signed onto his account, went back out to find Natalee, did what he wanted to her, and came back home thinking that he might be able to use the fact that he was signed onto the Internet as an alibi. After all, it seems to have worked.

Perhaps his brother Satish signed on for him and Deepak was not even home at all. But the story continues that Joran then text messaged the Kalpoe brothers at 3:00 a.m. to say that he had arrived home. Since any island video cameras on the route that Joran allegedly took on his walk home are only saved for a few days, by the time this particular story came out, we were told that the film had already been taped over—another missed opportunity for investigators to have obtained a piece of evidence, no matter how small, if only they had been diligent enough to begin the investigation right away.

Then we had the gardener who claimed to have seen all three boys in a car by the beach at around 2:30 a.m. He said they had tried to hide their faces from him. Why would they do that if they were just innocently hanging out together?

And, more importantly, we have Nadira Ramirez, the Kalpoe brothers' mother. She gave a statement on a taped interview with private investigators Harold Copus and John Weeks that was aired on the *Dr. Phil* television program on September 15, 2005. While having her face hidden for the interview, she said that she had returned to her home that she shares with the boys at twelve o'clock midnight on the night Natalee disappeared and they were not at home. She thought they returned around 3:00 a.m. and insisted that the reason she knew that was because she leaves her bedroom door open until the boys arrive home and they close it as a sign to let her know that they are there. After the investigators questioned her regarding how the boys had lied to her about taking Natalee back to the Holiday Inn, Mrs. Ramirez responded, "Come on, we all lie. We all lie. As big people, I know that I lie sometimes." After she realized that she had blown her sons' alibis, she desperately tried to get the tapes back and to keep the interview from being aired.

On that same program, another tape aired, this one was of Deepak Kalpoe. While in a hotel lobby in Aruba, Jamie Skeeters, President of the California Association of Polygraph Examiners, questioned Deepak while videotaping him. He asked the boy if he intentionally killed Natalee. Deepak responded, "No." Then Skeeters questioned him about whether the bartenders can be paid off to drug someone. Deepak responded, "I know there is a drug called Ecstasy. I heard they slip that into drinks." Skeeters also commented, "I'm sure she had sex with all of you." Deepak responded, "She did. You'd be surprised how simple it was."

Then the tape continued with Deepak discussing what he thought of Natalee: "To tell you quite frankly, dressed like a slut, talked like one. Would go in a car with three strange guys and her mother claiming her to be a goody two shoes. Enough of the BS already." This is an incredible contradiction coming from a boy who admittedly lied to the police . . . more than once. Natalee's dignity speaks for itself. There is not one thing in her life to indicate that she did not carry herself as a lovely, well-mannered, innocent, young woman. This may have been just one person's attempt to belittle his victim to justify his actions. The tapes have been the subject of much controversy as to their validity, as will be discussed later.

The boys' lies were out in the open. But there was so much more than the lies. Joran's reputation for womanizing, taking advantage of girls on their high-school graduation trips, putting belts around people's necks and simulating strangulation and then laughing about it, were all well-known on the island. His alleged proclivity for lying about anything he could to get close to the young girls he was trying to seduce, the stories about being a student visiting from Holland when, in truth, he lived there, were all familiar water cooler chatter. Yet his parents praised him. They covered for him, and his father, Paulus, was suspected of helping him to conceal the crime. As if that weren't bad enough, Paulus, a once alleged prominent attorney, counseled all three boys, Joran, Deepak, and Satish, about how to avoid prosecution, so much so that the chief prosecutor, Karin Janssen, considered his actions an obstruction of justice. Paulus denied any wrongdoing except to say that he did explain to his son some of the legal issues about being involved with this kind of case. Janssen claimed that the elder van der Sloot admitted telling his son, "Without a body, there is no case." But Paulus had told me at the prison that it was one of the attorneys who said that. I doubted that he was telling the truth. I had to keep in mind who we had been dealing with for the past few months. Joran was said to be a well-connected, spoiled kid whose father gambles with him and protects him, while his mother defends him and, at the same time, allows him to hang out in bars and casinos where he runs tabs and holds credit lines that make him look like a high roller. Whether true or not, he has gained a reputation that now precedes him. He knows he can get away with anything. We wonder why he does not worry about having to face the consequences for any of his actions. Maybe the following bit of information will help to explain that.

In early September 2005, an Amsterdam court sentenced eleven boys between the ages of fourteen and seventeen to up to twelve months in youth detention for gang raping three girls aged thirteen to fourteen. The last three months of the sentence were suspended, and ten of the boys were released immediately for time already served. They were also ordered into sexual behavior programs. The prosecutors had asked for the boys to be sentenced to a mere fifteen months. This is just an example of how lax the Dutch government seems to act when handling cases involving sex crimes against young females. In the United States, at the very least, the boys would have been sentenced to incarceration until they turned twenty-one for such heinous crimes.

And, if you add to the leniency the very real possibility that Joran may have connections inside of the Dutch hierarchy, then it is easy to understand why he might feel confident that he can do as he pleases without fear of consequences.

At times, the government seemed to follow suit with the suspects. Searches were impeded, and evidence was possibly moved from one place to another to a landfill, a beach, a pond, a lighthouse, a quarry, and God knows where else.

Segments of the government obviously knew more than they were willing to say. Aruba is very protective of their tourism industry, and they seem to wash anything that hurts their economy under the rug. Apparently, a judge's son is above the law. He went out with his buddies and they supposedly did something bad, and the police start their investigation by arresting everyone but them. But I had to try to look at this from their point of view in order to understand how this could happen. If I was one of those police officers working in that system and I go out and arrest a judge's son, what if I'm wrong? Since the blonde American girl did not come from Aruba, my best option is to protect the judge and my job, not the foreign girl.

In a place where power rules, it is hard to buck the establishment. I do not think that Aruba was ready for people like us. We swarmed the island, and others came in droves to help with our search. We never let up on them. We searched when they refused. We spoke out when they were silent. We did not back away and accept what they wanted us to believe, that Natalee's disappearance was of her own doing.

Our own search and investigation led us to some interesting information about the government some of which may or may not be credible. However, it left much food for thought, under the circumstances. Police Chief Jan van der Stratten is rumored to be Joran's godfather. At the very least, he is said to be good friends with Paulus van der Sloot. What an awkward position to be in when there is pressure coming at you from every direction to solve a crime your godson may have committed. His contract expired after Natalee's disappearance. There were rumors that he wanted to stay on the case, but that he was not allowed, so he went back to Holland. However, he was in Aruba at the police station with Dennis Jacobs when I was there in September 2005. After his contract expired, someone else was put in charge because of the way the investigation was going. It was a mess. The world had been allowed to see a different side of Aruba, one that had a great possibility of putting a large dent in their economy. That had to be stopped.

There were stories of conflicts between Prime Minister Nelson Oduber and Police Chief van der Stratten. Supposedly, Oduber couldn't get van der Stratten off the case immediately when he brought in the FBI, so he tried to fire van der Stratten when he flexed his muscles with the Dutch Marines. Apparently, the prime minister's responsibility was to approve paperwork regarding what the Dutch Marines could do on the island, but van der Stratten was the one who had the authority to give permission to let the island use the Dutch Marines for investigations the way they had in the past. However, this time, in Natalee's case, he supposedly did not allow them to do so, except on very specific searches, and he would only direct them to certain areas. I had to use the media to ask why the Dutch Marines had not been activated. The prime minister's response was that he had approved the paperwork, but it was the police chief who had control over activating them. They went back and forth with that, so Texas Equusearch came in to do their own search.

We also heard that the Deputy Police Commissioner Gerold Dompig is related to the Kalpoe brothers. His son told Beth that the Kalpoe brothers were his cousins. According to the Associated Press, Dompig was the one who originally claimed that one of the three suspects had confessed to killing Natalee. Then, Dompig retracted his statement. At one point, we had been told that he was no longer involved in Natalee's case, but apparently, he was later put in charge of it.

There had been so many stories and so much speculation that my head was spinning. Some things occurred that made me wonder if there was a reasonable explanation for them or whether there were people in the police department who were deliberately working against our best interests.

For instance, on June 2, 2005, during those first few days after

Natalee's disappearance, I had traveled to the California Lighthouse to initiate the land search with a group of approximately twenty to thirty tourists and locals. The lighthouse is elevated above the sand dunes. The Dutch Marines had been activated and were traveling to the area to conduct their own search. I was not aware they were going to show up. But I had to wonder if someone tipped them off that we were going to be in the area searching. Since it was still very early in the investigation, we did not realize that this area might have been part of a possible crime scene. Just as we were organizing at the lighthouse, my attention was diverted to a police car that had entered the sand dunes in the distance. The vehicle was crisscrossing through the dunes, making it appear as though a frantic search was being conducted. The car stopped by a huge boulder, but it was partially blocked from my view. *Did they find Natalee?* I wondered. My brother Phil and I noticed two police officers hurriedly looking around in the sand. The trunk of their car was open, but by the time we were able to get down there in the four-wheeler, the officers were getting back into their vehicle and leaving. I did not tell anyone else about this incident right away because it was the first day of our search and we did not have very many suspicions at the time. Subsequently, I reported the officers' strange activity to the FBI and asked that it only be reported to the chief of police and the prosecutor. In hindsight, I wonder if they had found Natalee buried in the sand and did not let us know. Or maybe they were looking for Joran's sneakers or some other evidence. It looked very suspicious. I later heard that a woman came forward who said that she heard about a policeman who helped dig up Natalee's body from the same area.

By June 11, 2005, we had searched most of the public ground areas. So, we rented a helicopter and flew over the island for approximately five hours. We covered all of the areas of the island that were visible from the air. We located some specific spots that required more attention. During our flight, we suddenly realized that a police chopper had been following us the entire time. I rented the helicopter on two other occasions and, both times, the police chopper shadowed our every move. The last time I was with Tim Miller from Equusearch, and he was amazed by their intrusive actions. Less than fifteen minutes into the flight, we decided to make a 180-degree turn and race back to an area we had missed. Upon receiving permission from the air traffic tower, we spun the chopper around and raced forward. In a few seconds, our helicopter and the police chopper were about to crash head-on. The police chopper took evasive action, and we slowed down. But the shadowing continued. I wondered why they felt the need to follow our every move. If we found something significant in Natalee's case, what would they have done? Were they afraid that we would find evidence that would implicate them, or were they more worried that we would solve the case when they were unable to?

Another interesting situation arose when the Noord Police Station was contacted by a tourist who indicated that she had found a bone with flesh in a snorkeling area near the lighthouse. She contacted them again one week later and they asked her, "Which bone? There are two." The tourist then notified me, and I in turn notified the FBI. The FBI agent brought it up at the next morning meeting and learned that the investigative team was unaware of either of the bones. He obtained the tourist's information, and we were told that a police officer had taken it upon himself to bring the bone she had found to a local medical facility. The person who was supposed to examine the bones was out on vacation for a week so there was a one-week to ten-day delay in the evaluation process. When they were finally analyzed, we were told that the fleshy bone was that of a donkey and the other was a large fish bone. I found the first set of results somewhat strange. Donkeys are known to stay on the other side of the island. I have never seen one of those animals near the location where it was found.

There was no indication of what they did with the bones after the lab was finished with them; they probably threw them in the garbage. It would have been prudent to hold on to them for verification purposes. After this incident, I wondered if this was the reason why the prosecutor wanted to personally take the duct tape with the blonde hair stuck to it to Holland, as evidence was not properly handled on the island. She had received a lot of ridicule regarding the medical person who had gone on vacation when the real reason for the delay may have actually been the poor handling of evidence.

In every situation, especially when a crime has been committed, people often give different versions of what happened, where there are little details that do not seem to match, but the big picture usually sounds fairly familiar. In this case, we are at a total loss, left with rumors, conjecture, hypotheses, hyperbole, theories, and whatever else we have been offered by mostly well-meaning individuals. We could not even get the three boys who were last seen with her to agree with each other. That was the most telling part of this ordeal. Surely, if they were all innocent, their stories would be in sync. Yet, we were expected to believe that there was no reason to be concerned about the fact that they told so many stories nobody could keep them straight, not even the boys. The inference was that the only way to actually convict someone in Aruba for committing a crime against Natalee would be to have a videotape of him committing the act. And, even then, I wonder what roadblocks we would face.

Since we were forced to gather our own information from the beginning and start our own search because the authorities would not comply, there is also the possibility that any evidence we might have found would have been considered tainted since we were not members of the police force. They might have said that there was no chain of custody or no way of knowing if we had planted something.

After all we had gone through, importing teams of professional searchers and coming up with the right type of machinery to look through a landfill for evidence when witnesses came forward pinpointing the spot where they saw a woman being buried, we felt as though we had been chasing a phantom. Maybe there was just nothing there to be found. Maybe she had been taken off of the island.

Over and over, we had leads that led nowhere; not a shred of solid evidence, not one single real clue; just the many different lies that the last three people to be with Natalee told. And that does not even seem to rise to the level of circumstantial evidence on the island of Aruba. But how circumstantial is it?

What about Joran's alleged statement that Natalee was going in and out of consciousness and that he may have committed a sexual assault? That, in and of itself, is problematic because Natalee would not have had the presence of mind to consent. In the United States, nonconsensual sex is considered rape. Reportedly, Joran even described her underwear in detail, which leads me to believe that he did violate her and that he must have seen her with the lights on rather than in the back seat of a dark car.

The boys acknowledged that Natalee was very intoxicated. Yet, they took no responsibility for whatever happened to her after they left her. Joran insisted that he walked away from her and left her alone on the beach. If any one of those boys were a decent human being, he would have made sure that Natalee was brought safely back to her hotel instead of talking badly about her and excusing himself for his own poor behavior.

All we had were rumors and lies. First, we were told that Natalee was hanging around with Joran, then that she rejected him. He stalked her; he hit her; she left Carlos'n Charlie's with him; she was tricked into getting into Deepak Kalpoe's car with him, thinking it was a taxi; she was looking for her friends and went back inside the bar, only to come back out being led by one of the Kalpoe brothers while she appeared to be in a drug-induced state; she wanted to be left alone on the beach; she was dropped off at her hotel and security guards helped her inside; she never showed up back at the hotel and her friends waited in the lobby until 5 a.m.

We seemed to always end up back in the same place: no answers, no trace of Natalee. What could we possibly do next?

SEVEN

The Two Faces of Paradise

AT FIRST GLANCE, OUR MIND SET WAS WHAT WE HAD
pulled up on the Aruba tourist Web site, "One Happy Island":
no crime, a very safe place. For the most part, that seemed to be
true and, at first, the authorities appeared to be doing whatever
they could to keep it that way. For one thing, it looked as though
most anything was legal there. *No wonder they are so happy and
consider the island crime-free,* I thought. They strive to be an
independent state, and that motivates them to hide their secrets,
such as rampant drug problems, alleged money laundering, and
rumors of powerful Mafia control. The different factions, coupled
with the Dutch influence, create a dichotomy, but an illusion of
harmony is reflected to keep the tourists coming. Until we saw the
conditions for ourselves, we had no way of knowing that we had
sent our child into such a dangerous environment.

Aruba's proximity to Venezuela and Colombia makes it much
too easy for the drugs to flow in and out. According to a 2003 U.S.
Department of Justice report, because Aruba is only about twenty
miles off the Venezuelan shore, it is a major hub for the transfer of
illegal drugs, the primary one being cocaine, but also heroin and
marijuana, which are abundant in Aruba. The report explains that
the drugs flow in and out of Aruba by air and sea, and while it is

distributed virtually all over the world, the majority of it ends up in the Netherlands. Due to the lack of import or duty tax in certain "free zone" areas in Aruba, there is no fear of any scrutiny from Aruban authorities. Thus, the drugs are freely moved in and out of the country. However, the drug trade is not the only illegal business that Aruba prospers from. According to the report, drug-related money laundering organizations also thrive in the environment due to bank secrecy laws as well as the stable currency.

There is a small investigative team of police or Politie in Aruba known as the Aruba Organized Crime Unit, which is responsible for investigating large-scale drug trafficking crimes. Then, there is the Coast Guard of the Netherlands Antilles and Aruba, known as the CGNAA. They are responsible for overseeing the maritime drug restrictions around Aruba and the Netherlands Antilles. The authorities of the Netherlands Antilles and Aruba have been joining forces with other coast guard units in the area to take a stand against drug trafficking.

The CGNAA has its own Criminal Intelligence Division, separate from the Aruba Politie. However, due to Dutch law, unless they can show that a specific ship is entering or leaving the territorial waters of the Netherlands Antilles or Aruba, it is illegal for them to take any action other than an administrative boarding. Thus, the waters are an easy escape for many of the drug traffickers and, I would assume, the sex trade traffickers, who frequent the area and know their way around.

After some more investigation, I found an article entitled "The Rothschild's of the Mafia on Aruba" by Tom Blickman, a researcher with the Transnational Institute's Drugs and Democracy Programme, which discusses Aruba. In it Blickman states that Aruba has a reputation as a "Mafia island," "which became public in March 1993 when it was described by the Italian daily

'Corriere della Sera' as 'the first state to be bought by the bosses Cosa Nostra.'"

It was with this in mind that I had remained cautiously optimistic about what the investigation that Aruban authorities were conducting into Natalee's disappearance would reveal. I was hoping that at least the prosecutor had been doing her best for Natalee, but now I cannot help thinking that there may be a few people involved in the investigation, or with enough influence over those who are, who cannot be trusted.

I realize that all countries are plagued with a certain amount of corruption, including the United States, and I am not one to rush to judgment about a place that I have so little knowledge of outside of my experience with Natalee's disappearance. But I am hard-pressed to wonder about the connection between the rampant drug trade and what happened to Natalee. Considering the recent rumors we heard about Natalee possibly being held somewhere as a sex slave, and that she may have been sold to pay off a gambling debt or a drug deal gone bad, how can I discount the possibility that she is another victim of what appears to be a well-known kidnapping ring whose predators search the islands for young vacationing girls who are far from home and vulnerable prey for these very experienced henchmen?

Most people are not aware of these facts when they peruse the beautiful travel brochures and Internet Web sites about Aruba and the surrounding paradise islands. These are not the areas of interest for a potential vacationer who is looking to travel to a foreign country and wants to feel safe. When browsing through the information, it is hard to believe that an island with that kind of reputation is able to keep such deep, dark secrets. Had we known that Aruba might be connected with such evil, we would have prevented our daughter from traveling there.

I have been told that Beth has received death threats. Why would anyone threaten a grieving mother and try to scare her off the island forever? I wonder if the answer is a simple one; maybe the publicity is harming their economy. Yet, I cannot believe that death threats would be warranted under those circumstances.

But I also find it hard to believe that with all of the press that Natalee's disappearance has attracted, there is not one person anywhere who knows what happened to her. I can only surmise that those who do know something are too afraid to come forward. Maybe there would be a price to pay if they tell, a price so high and so threatening that not even the $1,000,000 reward money is enough of an enticement for someone to bring us the truth.

Given all that we have heard, either there is some small-scale operation where the local boys chase after unsuspecting girls, drug and rape them the night before they leave, knowing that the girls will not press charges because they will be forced to stay on the island to pursue their case, or there is a much larger conspiracy where girls are made to disappear at the whim of some higher-ups who think the sale of a girl will earn them some good money. Whatever the case, it is unimaginable that nobody has one thing to say about a crime that is so blatant, so unsettling, so out-in-the-open that people from all over the world have gotten involved in an attempt to solve it, to no avail.

They say there is no perfect crime. So, I question how it is possible that three young boys could pull one off. I cannot help but wonder if the rumors about Paulus van der Sloot's involvement in Natalee's disappearance are true. He had his own problems; a story about him failing the test to become a judge, and we heard that he was really not as powerful as some people had implied. Maybe losing the opportunity to become a judge hurt him financially, or perhaps one of his alleged gambling jaunts went awry. But, if any of that is true, then why is there no evidence?

If three kids drugged and murdered Natalee, and a father showed up to dispose of the body in the middle of the night, something should have been left behind: a hair, a fingernail, a scratch, blood, anything that is usually found when someone commits an unplanned crime. Even those crimes that are meticulously premeditated do not escape all of the forensic specialists enlisted to solve them. So I believe that we might be talking about more than just three young boys and one father, all of whom may have gotten together in a frenzy to get rid of the evidence. I think there is much more to this story, and I am determined to find out what it is.

There are several people in the equation to consider besides the three boys and the father. There are also seemingly well-connected people who have been passing on leads and dropping hints. Sometime in early July 2005, Robin and I saw Deputy Police Commissioner Gerold Dompig's son and another young man who appeared to have similar descriptive features of Steve Croes, the *Tattoo* party boat disc jockey who had been arrested and released, trying to pick up a girl in the Holiday Inn lobby hallway and get her to go to Carlos'n Charlie's. The girl was offering resistance and trying to distance herself from those two. As the guys were walking by, young Dompig noticed me and immediately discontinued his activity. The other kid realized he was getting nowhere with the girl and started in on another set of young women. I walked up to Dompig, and he seemed a little embarrassed that we had witnessed his actions. He then started talking about the case, and during this conversation he mentioned that he had heard that Paulus van der Sloot had borrowed a friend's boat on either the night of Natalee's

Natalee, Class of 2005.

Matt, Brooke, and Natalee in a beach house
in Destin, Florida, August 2004.

Natalee's graduation night—our last
photo together.

Beach time in Florida with Matt and Natalee, August 2004.

Natalee and Brooke on graduation day.

Natalee and her Mountain Brook friends
in Aruba on the last day that she was seen.

Family photo of me, Beth, Brooke on
my shoulders, and Kaitlyn on my lap.

KIDNAPPED

LAST SEEN AT CARLOS & CHARLIES
MONDAY, MAY 29, 2005 1:30AM
NATALEE HOLLOWAY
CAUCASIAN AMERICAN FEMALE
BLUE EYES / LONG BLOND HAIR
5'4" 110 LBS.   18 YEARS OLD
ANY INFORMATION
PLEASE CALL 587-6222
OR CALL POLICE STATION 100

Natalee's missing person's poster.

Me and my father-in-law, Melvin Parten, during a search at the landfill.

Me searching on the landfill in Aruba.

Carlos'n Charlie's—the last place that Natalee was seen by her friends before she disappeared.

Aruban crack house and makeshift cardboard bed.

The fishermen's huts on the beach in Aruba.

Me, my brothers, Todd
Vestal and Phil Holloway,
and my sister, Linda Allison,
after a long day of
searching for Natalee.

After I, Patrick Murphy,
my brother, Phil, and
my brother-in-law,
Michael Parten (stand-
ing behind us), returned
from a day of searching
for Natalee, Robin
joined us for this photo.

My mother, Chris Holloway,
helping with our search.

My father-in-law with Greta van Susteren,
while taking a short break from searching.

Friends from Fox News in Birmingham, Alabama, came to Meridian
for an interview—Mai Martinez and cameraman, Kerry Nivens,
nicknamed "Care Bear."

The Florida State University Dive Team with me,
Robin, and my mom.

The California Lighthouse on Aruba.

A makeshift cross with the carved initials, N.H., that a tourist put up at the boat launch between the fishermen's huts and the Marriott Hotel where Joran said he left Natalee.

Me searching near the California Lighthouse.

disappearance or the next day and that he was allegedly involved with Natalee's murder. That brought to mind one of Joran's statements. He had referred to a friend by the name of Koen Gottenbos. Apparently, this friend's father owned a boat. The message was that this boat was used to take Natalee out to sea. Another boat that was also mentioned by him was the *Pair A Dice*, which is a local boat from Aruba.

The following evening, the same kid that was with Dompig was with another person, once again hawking girls in the lobby hallways of the Holiday Inn. Dompig was not present. We later saw the two meet up at a bar with a muscular black male, and it appeared that some sort of drug deal was being made. The black male exited the bar and headed to the beach area toward the Marriott Hotel. The two kids were then seen once again trying to very aggressively pick up young women. In one instance, the husband of one of the women intervened and asked the two kids to leave. The hotel does not like locals hanging around, but that didn't stop those boys from trying to scope the place for girls. I wondered if they were looking for potential victims for more than just their own entertainment. They were so obviously pressuring the girl that it seemed strange that they were merely looking for dates for the evening. Maybe there was more to their actions than a night out on the town. What if they were casing the place to find potential victims for sex slave traders? Or maybe they just felt free to do as they pleased because they knew that they could get away with it due to Dompig's connections.

Investigator Art Wood considered that there was sabotage all along in Natalee's case. He said he was told by one of the top detectives in the case that there was "a reliable lead that Natalee was being held in a certain house." The detective asked Wood to do surveillance there. When Wood responded that he thought it was a job for the police, the investigator commented that he couldn't trust his own officers. So, Wood searched the house, but he came up with nothing.

The following information is extremely curious to me, and it is something that has to be looked into further. It involves someone from inside of the Aruban Government. Apparently, in discussing what he considered to be a "blunder in Natalee's case," former Police Commissioner Stanley Zaandam said that the nomination of certain police commissioners, including Dompig, was against the law and the hierarchy of the KPA (police corp.), and that there were "serious consequences for the integrity and quality of the work in the KPA" due to that. He said, "None of the high-ranked commissioners has the qualifications nor experience to conduct a judicial investigation." He continued, saying, "This is how van der Stratten was appointed to this case." He maintained that Natalee's case was not the type of work in which van der Stratten should have been involved. However, he considers the biggest blunder to be the way the three boys, Joran van der Sloot and the Kalpoe brothers, were questioned, saying that their lies allowed them to remain free for twelve days. The part that most concerns me, though, was his statement that two days after Natalee's disappearance, her "body may have already been found and the police commissioner looked the other way to do a favor for Paulus van der Sloot. . . ." He continued that "to exculpate the son of Paulus, the police commissioner and the fiscal chief prosecutor . . . made the false arrest of two security guards, calling this a tactical maneuver. . . ."

So it seems as though something is unraveling from within, or maybe it is just the ramblings of an individual who might be a political foe of the current administration. Either way, it is more food for thought. But I still feel that this may all just be the tip of the iceberg.

Apparently, there is an undercurrent, a substratum of information that needs to be unveiled in order to uncover the truth. I have been peeling away at the layers very carefully trying to get to the core. If someone on the island is keeping everyone quiet with rewards for their silence, or through fear and intimidation, he or she is probably high up in the chain of command in some sort of hierarchy, whether it is the government or organized crime.

There has been a lot of speculation about that issue, so much so that the blogs and message boards have been filled with theories regarding who is responsible for what happened to Natalee. Her disappearance took on a life of its own on the Internet. Message boards were jammed with posts about her. As with our HelpfindNatalee@comcast.net address, some people just wanted to express their feelings, while others discussed what they thought had happened to her. However, among the latter group was also a subclass of people who began communicating in a language that was referred to as "code talking," which meant that they posted messages in a way that had to be deciphered to understand the true meaning. Most interpreted the codes as being filled with clues to the mystery we have all been trying to unravel: what happened to Natalee?

The most intriguing blogger was someone called "Shango." Shango became so well-known and had so many followers that his or her postings were known as "Shango's Riddles." Translating the riddles became a pastime for many bloggers. All sorts of interpretations were cropping up, but, after a while, there seemed to be an agreement that certain words were references to specific people, places, or things. While some of the language had us wondering, for the most part it soon appeared that the riddles left barely any room for interpretation.

Among code talkers, it was clear that they were all working off of a conspiracy theory. The riddles were being interpreted to mean that the people involved in Natalee's disappearance were high up in the chain of command on Aruba and in the Netherlands and that the rest of the islanders were afraid to come forward due to the power that those higher-ups possess.

Reading through the riddles and figuring out who the players were was like trying to solve the mystery behind the game Dungeons and Dragons, except, in this case, we were dealing with real life. And everyone seemed to have the same goal, solving the riddle and bringing Natalee home.

I have attempted to do my own interpretation of the riddle with some help from all I have read on the Internet, in e-mails, and on Natalee's Web site. I have put it all together in an appendix at the back of this book; it's lengthy but very intriguing. The lines of the actual riddle are underlined, and under each riddle, there are interpretations in parenthesis. Before the riddle is a key to what the words in the code might mean. All of it is open to interpretation, and nothing is meant to point the finger at any one person or group of people. It is all just suggestion and hypothesis, even though it tends to make a lot of sense. Check it out and see what you think.

It has been surmised that Shango knows a lot of information that outsiders were not privy to, and we consider this "Deep Throat" a possible source of pertinent information. Perhaps Shango is an insider in the government, or maybe he or she is a media person, like Jossy Mansur. Some of the comments would lead one to believe that somebody was feeding information to Shango or that he or she had instant access to it. It can also be suggested that Shango was one of the participants or close enough to them to know what actually went on the night Natalee disappeared.

Whoever you are, Shango, you apparently know more than you have revealed. Your riddles have been silenced, but we can still be reached at HelpfindNatalee@comcast.net.

EIGHT

The Media Spin

IT WAS THE END OF AUGUST AND NATALEE WAS STILL missing. Things were happening in Aruba that suggested that the truth was close to surfacing. Hurricane Katrina was upon us, and as I sat in the dark with no electricity, I began to analyze all of the events that had transpired. As I imagined all of the possible scenarios that could occur next, it was the furthest thing from my mind that a news satellite truck would come rolling into my driveway. The hurricane was in full swing, and the media was alive and well and attempting to come over to our house. Since we had been affected by the storm, Court TV called and asked Robin if we were okay. We thought that was very considerate of them, but then they asked if they could come over to interview us. A hurricane had just ravaged the South, and we had accepted the fact that some of the focus that had been on us for the past three months would turn in another direction for a little while. Considering the dire circumstances in New Orleans, I would never have expected the media to descend upon us while we were trying to survive our own situation in Mississippi. We were so grateful that they hadn't forgotten about us.

Much of the original response from the media when Natalee first disappeared was extremely supportive, but later things began to get somewhat out of hand. We had never dealt with the press before, and it was overwhelming to be faced with so many reporters at a moment's notice without knowing what we would be asked or what we should say. We just wanted to request help in finding our daughter, but when the investigation in Aruba began to unravel, the questions and answers were much different than anything we had originally anticipated. When Larry Garrison entered the picture, he advised us on how to handle the pressure of the media. Not only did he bring me information that others did not yet know, but he also positioned us effectively enough to keep Natalee's story alive.

During the hurricane, we could hardly communicate with the outside world. With no electricity and a bad cell phone signal, it was difficult to stay on top of what was happening in Aruba. We sometimes called Larry to find out what was going on. He was in touch with his colleagues in Aruba, and he was constantly checking the wires to keep us updated on the hearings for the three boys, Joran van der Sloot and Deepak and Satish Kalpoe.

When Hurricane Katrina first hit, we were asked by several networks to give interviews from my cell phone, but the reception was so bad that we decided to wait. However, once the hurricane turned into a major news story, we regretted not having taken that opportunity to speak to the press. Larry tried to set up some interviews for us. At that point, I was willing to go on the air from home to keep things alive even though we had no electricity. But Larry told me that he couldn't find anybody who was interested in talking to us. All of the news shows that had followed our every move only a day before had now become fixated on the next big ratings grabber: the victims of Hurricane Katrina.

Larry said that he had even tried to pitch to them that our story was tied in with the hurricane because we had suffered damage and were in the dark here in Mississippi, but he had no luck. It appeared that we were no longer a priority. We tried to understand, and we knew that the situation in New Orleans required the world's attention, but at the same time, we were afraid that Natalee would be forgotten. It was a learning experience for us. Watching the news, it's hard to grasp how it really works. But being the center of attention brings home the fact that news has to stay fresh and exciting, and it cannot remain focused on one thing for too long unless the circumstances continuously change.

The media never hesitated to ask us for an interview no matter what we were doing or where we were as long as it served their purpose of increasing ratings. But it also served our purpose of keeping our plight alive and informing the public that we needed help finding our daughter. Unfortunately, when things were happening in Aruba regarding the boys' detention hearings, the media was concentrating on the hurricane victims. That was frustrating for us because, as I will explain later, it was clear that the authorities had timed some of their actions to enable them to do things without the rampant publicity that had plagued them all summer long. Even though there were other important things going on in the world, I felt that a brief update from a hurricane survivor whose daughter was missing could find a small place in the news. I know it sounds selfish to have wanted some attention when so many people had been affected by the hurricane. I was only too aware of what everyone was dealing with even though we did not get the worst of the storm. We were left in the dark with many others, and there were numerous insurance claims from my clients piling up on my desk. I did my best to deal with them, but we still needed to know that nobody would forget about Natalee. We had to keep the story alive so people would come forward if they had any little bit of information that could help in our search for her.

But, due to the hurricane, the world had finally cut us off. The wrath of Katrina gave us momentary peace to sit in the dark and see what life was like without all of the commotion of the outside world. We had no Internet, no home telephone, no lights, no refrigerator, nothing to keep us informed about Aruba or New Orleans except those few cell phone calls we could receive. I had to keep my mind occupied. There was nothing I could do about Natalee, so I returned to my office and went over some of the insurance claims. I wondered if God was telling me that I needed to use the time I had now to get back in touch with my family here in Mississippi. I had been so consumed with the disappearance of Natalee and the difficulties that we endured with the Aruban government that this forced break brought some much needed quiet time for us. It was an opportunity for us to reflect on all that had happened, and in a way it was a respite for Robin. One of the issues that had come up for us was that she is reserved, and it was difficult for her to do interviews on national television. But it was for Natalee, and because of that, she agreed to do them even though it was very painful for her to sit in front of the world and speak. The only thing I can say is that when there is a purpose, a valid motive, it is easier to overcome fears that you normally are not able to walk through.

When the hurricane became less of a news focus and we were back on track with our quest for the truth about Natalee, the media came through and followed our story, once again.

However, at times, it was hard to tell the difference between members of the press who were sincerely interested in helping us find Natalee and those who were mainly looking to increase their ratings. I suppose it did not really make a difference as long as we were getting the publicity that would help us find our daughter and bring those responsible for her disappearance to justice. While we appreciated every bit of airtime that we were allotted, we were also exposed to some things that we had never anticipated.

From the moment that Natalee had disappeared, our phones began ringing off the hook. The questions were never ending. I was somewhat naïve in believing that the press would always consider our best interests above all else, that they would understand the torture we were experiencing and that they would do whatever they could to help Natalee. I had never imagined the way the media actually works behind the scenes. I often felt as though I were caught in the middle of a tug of war. Everybody was fighting for exclusives. Many members of the press attempted to endear themselves to us in the hopes that we would talk to only them and shut everyone else out. Some people said whatever they could whenever they could in an effort to gain another story about Natalee. All we were concerned with was getting our daughter back. We realized that as time passed, the story would lose momentum. It was the natural order of the news. Something else would happen, and the focus would shift away from us once again. So we made it our campaign to do everything we could to keep her story alive. But it hasn't been easy.

When we first arrived in Aruba, we met Carla. She was the woman who had tried to stop us from searching at the California Lighthouse. She told us that she worked for the company in charge of publicity for tourism in Aruba and that it was her job to help us coordinate with the press. Carla offered to be the Holloway family spokesperson and, being new to all of this, we agreed. We felt relieved to have someone take charge of this unknown territory for us. At first, she seemed quite helpful, but it became obvious to us that members of the press were unhappy with the fact that she had total control over who could interview us. We felt that everything she was doing was in our best interest.

At one point, she arranged for us to do a *20/20* segment, then she insisted that we do it as an exclusive with them. That meant we would not be able to speak to anyone else. Even though we believed that it would benefit us to speak with anyone who would listen, we hesitantly agreed with Carla, thinking that she knew best. All we really cared about was finding our daughter.

Our first indication that something was amiss was when she tried to stop our search at the lighthouse. She had discussed it with Beth and then came back to me instructing me to call it off. As previously mentioned, we went ahead with that search. The decision to call off a search for my daughter was not about to be determined by a publicity person. I immediately set her straight and told her that I do not take orders from anyone. At that point, it was already obvious that we were not working as a team. The following week, Carla came to me with tears in her eyes. She said that her bosses were reassigning her to another location because the Aruban government felt that she was promoting our side more than theirs. I think it was God's way of allowing us to take back control of our situation. From that moment on, Robin and I decided to speak out on every show possible. We had our hands full. We were trying to decipher the reports that were coming to us from the FBI, and the Aruban prosecutor's office and family members were working hard to help us stay visible in the news.

Whether I was in Aruba or Mississippi, it was amazing how the press would somehow always manage to find me. At a memorial football game at my daughter's school, the media contacted us several times for interviews when Deepak and Satish were re-arrested with their friend Freddy. I was sitting there in the middle of the game on the phone with *Larry King Live*, Rita Cosby from

MSNBC, and others from various news outlets. The next morning, Robin and I appeared on *Good Morning America*, *The Today Show*, and some others. I found out later that the ratings were so high on the stories about Aruba and Natalee that CBS and ABC were pooling the news to cooperate with each other. I wondered if it was the public that had an insatiable appetite for her story, or was it being force-fed to them by the media? But I honestly did not care about the answer as long as we could keep the story in the forefront for Natalee's sake.

At times, we got calls from members of the press telling us stories about events that had not actually occurred. We assumed that they were fishing for information and trying to prompt us to talk to them by discussing various suspicions that had been raised. But then there were reporters like Geraldo Rivera's brother, Craig, who offered to accompany us to investigate leads and ended up being very helpful when we thought we were in a jam at the VIP Club.

Due to our previous experience with Craig, we were willing to help him and Geraldo when they asked for our assistance on a story. On Saturday, June 11, 2005, they wanted us to take them to Carlos'n Charlie's to show them how prolific the drug trade there was. Robin and I declined, but Michael, Phil, and Linda went with them in the hopes that they would use what they saw to show the world that there was more to this "One Happy Island" than the brochures and Web sites were revealing. Craig set up a camera, and Phil walked to a street corner. He looked across the street and gave a mere nod of his head. Several drug dealers were there. The first guy ran across the street to where Phil was. Phil simply opened his hand, and the dealer placed a sizeable amount of cocaine in it and stated that it would cost $120. Phil told him to take the cocaine back. The guy asked him,

"What are you, the FBI, you FBI, you FBI?" Phil said, "No. There's a guy over there filming us." The dealer said, "Oh, okay. Well, then, let's just walk around the corner where he can't see you." Of course, Phil did not go any further with the guy. But Geraldo and Craig got enough for their story, and we felt comfortable helping them. So in that case, it was a give-and-take situation with the press.

News show host Alan Colmes from *Hannity and Colmes* was kind enough to go on searches with us, but he became too uncomfortable from the desert-like conditions. The heat took a lot of getting used to, especially in the areas where we were searching during the hottest part of the day.

Some reporters went to extremes doing anything and everything they could to get close to us and learn details before anyone else. For instance, when the pond was being drained, two reporters started fighting with each other for a chance to interview me. It became so uncomfortable that I had to leave.

There were times when I suspected that some of the news media were creating situations just for attention. For instance, an arm that turned out to be nothing more than a Halloween prop had been found off the coast of Venezuela, and everyone was in an uproar as to whether it was Natalee's. I couldn't help but wonder whether the press or some sick person merely looking to create publicity had planted it.

Another situation came up one day when we were searching on the opposite end of the island from the Holiday Inn. We received word that the police had roped off the area just north of the Marriott Hotel. Curiosity and a much-needed break lured us back to the area just to see what was going on. We made the mistake of parking our vehicle and walking between the police line and the road up to the area in question. The path was the width of a sidewalk. Suddenly, the press spotted us and came running at us. There were several cameramen and about a half dozen microphones being pushed in my face. The area was so constricted that two of the cameramen actually got into a shoving match. Thankfully, the scuffle was short lived. Questions were being shot at me from all sides. There was so much commotion that I could not understand what anyone was saying. One of them asked what we thought about some clothing and condoms that were found. I commented that we had already searched the area and the island is littered with various articles of clothing and other things. "That's not so unusual," I added. We then turned and left. We had arrived there thinking that something significant must have been discovered due to the way the press was swarming the area, but it was just another false alarm

Once Robin and I began to realize that the press was hungry for a story, any story, we were very careful not to release any pertinent information that might have compromised the case. We also knew we had to pace ourselves and not get too excited about anything we heard unless and until we saw something big happening with our own eyes.

A few days after the incident by the Marriott Hotel, I was in the lobby of the Holiday Inn preparing to leave for a search when I received a call from our FBI liaison telling me that the police were making plans in the event that the family needed to be notified if Natalee was found. Someone either overheard the conversation or else the line was tapped because as I walked out of the building to continue the conversation with more privacy, someone came up to me and asked if I was on my way to identify a body. When I went back inside the hotel and up to my sister Linda's room to get something, the TV was on, and I noticed that it was already on the news that I was on my way to identify a body. I was shocked to see how quickly *and inaccurately* some members of the media were occasionally able to work.

As the time passed, we were appearing on every news show imaginable. We were even booked to appear on *Larry King Live* three times in one week. It was far beyond our expectations. I felt that it was only right to speak out to all of the news outlets in case the public wanted a broad perspective and to reach anyone who might stay with a particular news network. We wanted to make sure that we reached as many people as possible because we did not want to take the chance that someone with important information might not be aware that we needed it.

While I was learning how the news media in the United States worked, I found out that the Aruban government and all three suspects also had their own spin machines. People were posting blogs all over the Internet about them, and my stomach would turn reading what their supporters had to say. I also cringed when I heard that trips to Aruba were being given away on shows like *Live with Regis and Kelly*. I wondered if the Aruban government had arranged that to reactivate interest in tourism. I wanted to warn people about the real dangers there. Looking back, I am sure Regis and Kelly were not even aware of the implications.

We always had to think carefully about what we would say to the media and not allow our emotions to carry us away with comments we might regret later. We were angry and disappointed with the Aruban government, but we did not want to speak badly of them because we felt that would be defeating our purpose. We were also careful not to be too severe when discussing the suspects because, even though we felt in our hearts that they had more information than they were giving up, we didn't want to make it look like we were on the attack and just interested in finding someone, anyone, to hold responsible for Natalee's disappearance;

besides, it is possible that they were not responsible and we didn't want to cast false aspersions.

When we had developed the e-mail address that people were sending all sorts of comments and leads to about Natalee, we were hoping to introduce it on *Larry King Live*, and we had made it clear before the interview that we would like to let everyone know about it. However, it was hard to know when and if the time was right for the subject to be brought up. We somehow managed to discuss it, but we felt lucky to have fit it into the conversation. Sometimes, we knew ahead of time what the questions were, while at other times, we didn't have any idea which way an interview was going to go. We have been on news programs where the interviewer had an agenda and only wanted specific answers for his or her questions. We realized that the real motive was to pry for more information that others did not yet know. We would answer a question with a tiny detail and then try to lead the interviewer in another direction. We did not always succeed, but that works both ways. I did not always give them what they wanted either. I was certainly not too bashful to say, "It would hurt the investigation to answer that now."

Some of the interviews we did were via satellite. It is very challenging. The interviewer would be in another location, and we would be sitting in a small room wearing an earpiece and looking into the camera. Lights would shine in our eyes, and the feed on the television monitor was delayed so the words were not in sync with the questions. We were told to look into the camera or just below it and not into the delayed television monitor. We would then answer the questions while hearing them. It was difficult not to look up, which we were told would take the viewer's attention away from our statement.

We quickly learned to be direct and answer with authority. We are not professionals, and given our circumstances, we hope the public takes that into consideration. Nobody expected perfection, and we felt that the more genuine we were, the easier it would be for people to relate to us. We felt we were fighting against corruption and a spin from people who can get very ugly, so it was important to be clear, concise, and honest. We always portrayed the truth to the best of our ability and hoped that others might be influenced to come forward to aid us in finding out what happened to Natalee.

The entire experience was a drain. For the life of me, I will never understand why some members of the press had no problem calling us for a scoop at all hours of the night, but then they would get angry because we were worn out and did not have the energy for an interview. However, most of the media were respectful of our need for some privacy and downtime.

There were times when the media twisted my words. I would tell them something and hear it coming back a completely different way. I suppose they have to do what they can to boost ratings, but I feel that letting the truth be known has to be more important than that.

Often, newscasters ran to Aruba to set up shop in order to be the first out of the box with information. I was surprised when NBC was able to gain access to the prison and tape Joran. According to the Aruban authorities, their actions could have jeopardized the criminal case against him if his attorney made a case for the violation of his rights. Thankfully, no one forced the boy to speak. However, the warden spoke out about Joran's anger problems and was obviously not a fan of the van der Sloots so it was not a big shock when he was fired after allowing the NBC crew access to the prison.

Many members of the media truly appeared to care about us. It was comforting to hear from a member of Larry King's staff who called during the hurricane to see if we were okay. We were truly touched by that. Others allowed us to say whatever we needed to and went out of their way to respect our privacy. We even traded information with a producer at NBC. Sometimes he would tell me about rumors that he had heard about the boys and Carlos'n Charlie's, and I would let him know which ones were true. He even talked about going into the bar undercover with a camera for NBC.

After setting up our e-mail addresses about Natalee, news shows helped us by advertising them. We were also able to ask the public for financial assistance through these media outlets. Appearing live on television afforded us the ability to say what we wanted without fear of being edited. Doing our campaign for justice allowed us to fight back against the spin of the Aruban government and the boys, while also putting pressure on them. Those in Aruba did not seem to recognize that our family, our daughter, was violated. We would not stand for that. We knew the truth about Aruba, and we wanted everyone else to understand what we had been dealing with. So we revealed the existence of Aruban crack houses to the press. We educated people about the rampant use of date rape drugs and ecstasy in Aruba and the lax attitude about what minors traveling to their island were allowed to do. This isn't the paradise it's painted to be, and parents should be concerned about the high possibility that their children will get mixed up in sex, drugs, and maybe even violence. As if that weren't bad enough, it looked more and more to us like these things were happening in a place of blatant corruption where crimes are seemingly covered up. The island boys may be getting away with rape and murder.

We had every right to seek justice and do everything we could to find our daughter. When the Kalpoe brothers were released, we showed our outrage to the world and put pressure on the Aruban authorities to investigate them further. Did they really believe that we would just slink away like the young girls who reportedly had been used and abused the night before they left the island and were afraid to lodge a complaint? They didn't have the where-withal to fight back from thousands of miles away, but with the media's help we could keep the heat on like they couldn't.

It amazes me how long some people are able to hold back the truth, but we see it every day. One person finally comes out and reports a crime, and suddenly several other victims come forward. It isn't a coincidence that those crimes often involve sexual abuse. People often feel humiliated and fear the type of negative public-ity that rape victims often face. Their silence comes from either fear and shame, or, in the case of Aruba, it is possible that the cor-ruption and cover-ups that are so rampant there keep people from coming forward with the truth. If someone does speak out, they have no way of knowing what the repercussions will be, especially in a place like Aruba. But we were too big for them. We brought everyone we could with us. We bombarded the world with Natalee's story. We were not afraid. There were too many of us and too many members of the press who were willing to pay attention to our plight. The spin may have gone out of control at times, but we were always able to pull it back in and gain momen-tum. Larry Garrison had a handle on the press. He guided us and paved the way for some of our most important interviews. We were grateful to have someone like him on our side, and sure enough, after the news coverage of Hurricanes Katrina and Rita waned, we were back on the air keeping Natalee's story alive.

In all of our turmoil, one thing has been a constant for us. We will continue to seek justice for Natalee. We will balance our lives in a way that allows us to continue our search for her. I honestly believe that God does not give us more than we can handle. We all have a purpose on this earth. Maybe it was Natalee's destiny to bring out the truth of corruption on that little island. Hopefully, the press coverage about her will save at least one other person from suffering her fate. Whatever the media really is, either a vehicle with which we are able to tell our tale or a spin machine that tales are made from, it has been essential in getting the story out to the public and keeping it in the forefront for such a long time.

Media coverage has enabled Natalee to become a symbol for every child in the world. Though some might view her as just another blonde, white, American girl to whom the media tends to pay more attention than minorities, people of every race and religion have come forward to extend to us compassion and understanding. Natalee's story has touched everybody in a special way. The media allowed her into everyone's homes and everyone's hearts. This tragedy could have happened to anyone's child, black, white, rich, poor, Christian, Jewish, Muslim, whatever. There are no lines to be drawn when it comes to a parent losing a child. Hopefully, the media has brought that home to the world.

NINE

Putting the Pieces Together

ON AUGUST 26, THE FBI CALLED TO INFORM US THAT the Kalpoe brothers had been arrested again along with Joran's friend, Freddy Alexander Zedan-Arambatzis, twenty-one, who was brought in for suspicion of another crime unrelated to Natalee. He had a Web site on which he called himself the "Locoman Pimp." He was accused of taking photos of a minor female in "tempting poses" and showing them to other people. He was further suspected of having unspecified "physical contact" with the girl. The Kalpoe brothers and Joran were also considered suspects in the incident, which had occurred prior to Natalee's disappearance. This news was promising to us. We felt that it would put more pressure on Joran, and it might be what was needed for him to finally tell the truth.

Apparently, Deepak had heard that his alibi had been compromised by the gardener who witnessed the boys in Deepak's car on the night of Natalee's disappearance. So, he contacted a girl he knew and tried to convince her to say he was with her. Instead, she contacted the FBI. We heard that this was why Deepak was arrested the second time. Prior to the arrest, Jamie Skeeters had attempted to convince Deepak to take a lie detector test because he had heard about the girl and was hoping that Deepak's failed attempt at getting an alibi would influence him to tell what he knew. Unfortunately, the arrest put an end to that idea.

As always, news of more arrests in the case traveled quickly, and the airwaves buzzed with interviews. Once again, Jossy Mansur revealed an interesting scoop of his own when *Scarborough Country*'s Lisa Daniels asked him his opinion about the four boys now in custody. He responded, "These four guys are friends. They belong to the same group, these party boys that go out and prey on young, unsuspecting girls or other kinds of girls also that are out to have a good time, not suspecting what they're in for with these predators around. And they are, they not only appear in photographs together, but I understand that Freddy lives very near to the Joran house. So there is a bond between them. There is a group that they call themselves the pimps, in which all of these participate." Jossy always managed to stay one step ahead of the rest on the island when information was needed. Hearing what he had to say was unsettling, but we felt that the more boys involved in the publicity surrounding Natalee's disappearance, the more likely it was that one would talk.

We were told that the Kalpoe brothers were being held on suspicion of rape and murder in Natalee's case. According to Prosecutor Janssen, they were suspected of the "primary criminal act of together with other people committing premeditated murder, alternately together with other people, murdering somebody, more alternately rob a person of her liberty with fatal consequences and even more alternately raping somebody." We knew that there had to be new facts and circumstances to rearrest the Kalpoe brothers.

We were encouraged. We assumed that the Dutch interrogators must have finally been able to get tangible evidence. They could not afford to make any mistakes with those boys. Prosecutor

Janssen felt good about the case too. In fact, she was so confident that she bypassed the first ten days of normal detention, and the court ruled that they could go right into pretrial stages where additional DNA and other evidence could be obtained. We were not given any details regarding the evidence, but Robin and I felt certain that the case was moving forward at a faster pace now.

That morning, we were happy. Other than bringing Natalee home alive, the arrests were the best news we could have gotten. We didn't think that the Kalpoe brothers would have been brought in if there were not sufficient reason. We also felt more confident about Joran's upcoming hearing on September 4, 2005. We were sure that he would be detained longer now. My mother was hopeful too. She had been going through this with us. She came to Aruba and saw how hard the Aruban people worked to help us. At the time, she believed that the Aruban authorities were doing all they could and were working very hard to find Natalee. She has managed to keep her strength, as we have, through her faith in God and prayer.

As encouraging as all of the recent news was, the feeling that we were finally getting somewhere did not last very long. In the midst of Hurricane Katrina, the three suspects, Joran van der Sloot and Deepak and Satish Kalpoe, were released. It happened on September 2, 2005; a judge first ordered the three boys to remain in custody longer: the two boys for another eight days and Joran, another thirty days. To our surprise, he immediately suspended their detentions and ordered that they all be released on condition that the Kalpoe brothers not leave the island and Joran not leave Dutch territory. In addition, all three were to remain available to authorities investigating Natalee's disappearance. Larry was the first person to reach us with the news that the judge ordered the boys to be released and that the prosecution planned to appeal the judge's decision. Robin cried when she heard about the boy's pending release. It was a setback for us, but we were getting pretty familiar with setbacks in Natalee's case by then.

Hurricane Katrina had left the door open for the boys to be sent on their way with little publicity and few restrictions because it took the world's focus off of Natalee, but only for a brief time. The huge amount of publicity that we had been receiving for Natalee's disappearance had waned and, during that time of quiet for us, Joran and the Kalpoe brothers were sent home.

Apparently, when Joran was about to be released, the authorities had planned to wait until the middle of the night because a mercenary had threatened to kill him. Instead, the authorities felt it would look bad to sneak him out, so they had police on top of the buildings watching for snipers when they set him free.

The prosecutor immediately appealed the judge's decision to release the boys and the Court of Appeals had to arrange a date for hearings. Joran's lawyer announced that, as a Dutch citizen, Joran would be allowed to go off to Holland to start college. At some unknown time prior to this, Freddy had been quietly released without charges being brought.

During the boys' confinement, I had a conversation with the prosecutor and told her "not to file charges unless they were sure they had enough evidence to convict." If that meant waiting awhile longer, then we would be patient. If the boys are charged with a crime and, during the trial, the judge rules there is insufficient evidence to convict them, then they cannot be retried for the same offense because of double jeopardy. While we were anxious to see the case move forward with some speed, at the same time, I knew that they had to be extremely careful so as not to hinder the investigation in any way.

On September 9, 2005, the appeal was heard regarding overturning the suspension of the boys' detention. If the judge over-turned it, Joran would have to return to Aruba to serve another thirty days in jail and the Kalpoe brothers would have to finish out their eight days. Prosecutor Janssen had also asked that the boys be compelled to give DNA samples. We hoped that enough evidence had been presented to force the judge to comply.

On Wednesday, September 14, 2005, the Aruban Court of Appeals dealt a blow to us when they ruled that Joran van der Sloot and Deepak and Satish Kalpoe, the three main suspects in Natalee's disappearance and the last people to be seen with her, could now remain free without any of the restrictions with which they were originally released. The ruling came because there was a "lack of sufficient grounds and serious suspicions" to keep the conditions on the three boys.

Robin and I were disappointed in the judge's decision to release the boys. We were even more astounded to hear that all of the restrictions on the boys were to be lifted. We were back at square one once again. We decided to focus on the long term, and although we had been dealt another blow, the time period to file charges was still alive. We may have lost another small battle, but the war was far from over.

Shortly after the three main suspects were released, Prosecutor Janssen once again requested a search of the pond north of the Marriott Hotel that firemen had previously drained. Early in the morning on Labor Day weekend, they began draining it and came up with several items, including a pocketbook filled with rocks that also contained a headband. Obviously, the rocks were an attempt to keep the pocketbook at the bottom of the pond. Also found were two cloth bags, a shoe, a machete, and two pieces of drug paraphernalia. The items were supposed to be examined to see if they had a connection to Natalee, and the prosecutor was going to request that the judge require more DNA samples from the suspects. However, I was subsequently told that Natalee only had $50 and her driver's license with her when she left her hotel room on the night of her disappearance. I was doubtful that the pocketbook had anything to do with her.

I wondered if it was just a mere coincidence that none of us were there to watch the digging this time. And the fact that the boys slithered out of prison during a hurricane that took the media's focus off of Natalee's story—was that another coincidence? Was the plan to send them home when no one was watching? Maybe they thought the media attention would never come back, and they could sweep the whole nasty incident under the rug where they thought it belonged. It seems to me as though that was the plan from the beginning. The "One Happy Island" conspiracy, as I call it.

The boys were free, the press was barely visible, the hurricane was becoming old news, the hours had become days, then weeks, then months, and we had no idea where to look next.

Joran was in Holland at college, and our thoughts turned to Natalee and all of the hopes and dreams she had. She would have been at college now too, happily preparing for her future. We would have been receiving updates on how she liked it, who her new friends were, what activities she was involved in, and what her roommate was like. We heard that her roommate was saving her bed for her in the hopes that she is brought back to us alive. Meanwhile, Joran's life was moving along as he had planned, and rumors were still flying. Some people said that he was up to his old tricks, cutting school, staying out all night, drinking, partying, and going after girls. I suppose his notoriety could go both ways for him. Young impressionable girls might believe in his innocence and like the fact that he is famous. Other kinds of girls might get excited over going out with a "bad boy."

In late September 2005, a producer for the television show *A Current Affair* approached Joran at college in Holland. In his usual arrogant demeanor, Joran was at first adamant about not wanting to be interviewed, but he did not hesitate to continue talking. While it is likely that he had been instructed by his parents and his legal counsel not to say anything more about the case, he could not seem to help himself. Standing in front of what appeared to be his college campus, he casually told the producer, "I knew her for one night. I feel horrible that I even went out that night without my father knowing. I should have just stayed home and this wouldn't have happened to me. It would happen to another person. I just try to look at it that I was at the wrong place at the wrong time, maybe even with the wrong people. And I just hope that the truth comes out, that th[ere] comes some clarity in the case."

Here is my response to that statement. His main concern is about what happened to him. He shows no compassion for Natalee. This is all about him being in the "wrong place at the wrong time." If I were in his shoes, and if I had really left Natalee alone on the beach, I would be kicking myself over the fact that I could have done something that would have prevented any harm from coming to her. This is, of course, not the same situation as the acquaintance of Natalee's who saw her walking out of Carlos'n Charlie's. He felt responsible for not having stopped her from leaving with Deepak, but he had no way of knowing that she was in danger. However, when you look at what Joran did, that is a whole different story. When you leave an intoxicated girl on a dark, desolate beach in the middle of the night, you have to know that she is in danger. So, I if I were being interviewed and my worst offense were leaving Natalee alone, I would start by apologizing to her family and asking for forgiveness for making such a terrible judgment call. I would not be standing there arrogantly acting as if this whole ordeal was about my own bad experience. He has had that attitude from the very beginning when we first arrived in Aruba, so he cannot even explain it away by saying that he had enough of us or that he is angry at having been locked up in prison all summer.

If I were in his situation, then I suppose I would have done exactly what Joran did, deflect the attention and concern away from Natalee and her family and put myself in the position of being the victim. It could work for him.

I wonder why Joran has never seemed to be the least bit afraid that all of his lies would eventually catch up with him. As the interview in Holland continued, he did not even flinch when he stated to the interviewer, "We agreed to lie," we, meaning he and the Kalpoe brothers. He then repeated one of his many stories, saying that he left Natalee on the beach: "She wanted to stay here the whole night. I told her no I had to go. I even lifted her up to carry her back to the hotel, and she told me to put her down. I had school the next day. I told her I had to leave and she didn't want to listen. So basically I thought okay, then if you want to stay here, then you stay here, and that is the truth."

He went on to say that they had been drinking together: "Obviously, she was drunk. I had stuff to drink too. She wanted to go with me. I wanted to go with her. It was totally consensual."

When the producer asked Joran if he had sex with Natalee, his first response was that it was "none of your business." But again he went on to answer, saying that none of the boys had sex with her.

I could not help but feel that Joran's statements were all part of his overall plan. He made up the story to protect himself, and I saw right through him. He said that none of them had sex with Natalee. However, prior statements indicate otherwise. He previously stated that he had sex with her while she was going in and out of consciousness. But in Holland he stated, "She wanted to go with me. I wanted to go with her. It was totally consensual." What does he mean by that? Is he saying that he did not kidnap her and take her to the beach against her will because she consented to go? Or is he saying that they had sex and it was consensual, even though they were both drunk? What exactly was the consensual part he was referring to?

Joran went on in the Holland interview to explain what he would have done differently that night: "I would have just stayed home that night. I wouldn't have even gone out. It was Natalee who asked me to go out with her. It was her that asked me to come to the club. And it was her that was yelling at me to go dance with her, and I said—and I went to go drink something with my friends."

We knew that Joran disobeyed his parents and snuck out of the house. We knew that he was in the casino gambling even though he was underage. He was also drinking in the bar even though he was underage, and he expected us to believe that he was an innocent and that Natalee lured him out and caused this whole ordeal.

After the interview, it seemed as though people believed that there had been a huge revelation because Joran admitted on television that he and the Kalpoe brothers "agreed to lie." But we always knew they had lied. It was not our opinion. It was fact. The differences between all of his accounts of the events are so evident and so telling in that we all know that the truth has only one version. How do you tell several different versions of what is supposed to be the same story and not be lying? The words came out of his mouth when the cameras were on him, and I suppose, for those viewers who had not been following the story closely enough, it looked like something big had happened. But the truth is that Joran was just repeating what everyone involved in the case already knew: he's a liar.

Joran is not the only deceitful person involved with this case. We knew that the Kalpoe brothers lied. Their mother admitted that she lies. Paulus was caught in a lie when he said he picked his son up at 11:00 p.m. on the night of Natalee's disappearance after several people heard him say it was at 4:00 a.m. the following morning. But can we trust what the rest of the participants in this drama did?

The FBI was called in to help with Natalee's case from the very beginning, a noble gesture on the part of the prime minister. But was that all it was, a gesture, just another tactical maneuver to keep us thinking that the case was being taken seriously? After all, the FBI's hands were tied. They had no access to any records or files. Was their invitation to Aruba simply for show?

I must also comment on Prosecutor Janssen's sudden trip to the Netherlands in the middle of the investigation. I do not think I was alone in my feeling that it was a poor choice of timing for her to fly off to visit her family. As a matter of fact, there were others who openly agreed with me. Fox News's Greta van Susteren had this to say:

> Now the chief prosecutor is on a two-week vacation to the Netherlands! I don't know what you think . . . but it seems to me that if you are in charge of the only murder investigation in your country, and if the clock is winding down on holding your chief suspect, that you might want to delay that vacation a few weeks. Even some of us worked vacation days covering the story and we are not in charge of the investigation . . . we are simply covering it for a news organization. You cannot blame a prosecutor or a police chief if a crime is perfect and not provable, but I do think it

is fair to criticize them for taking a vacation mid-investigation when there is a clock running.

To be fair, there were suggestions that this was a "working vacation." Lead Prosecutor Janssen was supposedly escorting the duct tape with hair and the DNA saliva samples all the way to the lab in the Netherlands herself, but it seemed strange that there was absolutely nobody else in the prosecutor's office that could be trusted to transport a small sealed bag of evidence to its destination while keeping the chain of custody intact. I wondered what that indicated about the trust within the department. On the other hand, Prosecutor Janssen did remain in the Netherlands for two weeks, and she was staying with relatives. So, I suppose it is possible that she combined work with her vacation time. After all, there doesn't seem to be any other reason for her to hang around the Netherlands for two weeks waiting for the lab results when they could have been faxed back to Aruba.

The witnesses were another story. One temporarily disappeared after bravely coming forward with eyewitness testimony. Another supposedly failed a lie detector test. And another was allegedly put in a mental institution. Was the purpose of all of those witnesses to keep us running back and forth all over the island in a desperate hunt for Natalee while she was being smuggled out of the country or while evidence was being destroyed? There has to be a good explanation for so many false leads.

What about former Police Commissioner Stanley Zaandam? He has commented that Natalee's body may have been found and the current police commissioner looked the other way as a favor to Paulus van der Sloot. He added that the prosecutor and police commissioner also falsely arrested the two security guards to exculpate Paulus's son, Joran, the main suspect. It was supposedly a "tactical maneuver." I guess that is the new term for creating a diversion in order to give suspects a chance to cover up a crime.

I have also considered the possibility that all of the arrests and releases of the suspects were done for effect to kill time. Maybe the authorities thought that if they made us feel as though they had solved the case, we would let our guard down a little, stop focusing on other possibilities, and go home. And, with all of the searching that we did, they most likely thought that we would finally see that there was nothing to be found on their island and we would throw our hands up in the air and give up.

One more thing to consider: it appears to be a well-known fact that in Aruba, contracts are handed out in exchange for favors, and payoffs are commonplace to get jobs done without any interference. For example, one local U.S. contractor told me that he was in charge of a construction project in Aruba. He quickly realized that there were going to be cost overruns. He said that many of the officials had to be paid off in order to get anything done. His boss knew this and told him not to worry about it. That was just the way it is in order to do business in Aruba. "That was to be expected," he said. Also, while I was searching at the landfill, I was told that when the bids came up, a bid that was several million dollars higher than a competing one was accepted. It was later determined that the high bidder was a relative or close family associate of the person in charge of the bid process.

Taking that into consideration, I look at Paulus van der Sloot, a one-time judge-in-training who flunked out and went back to Holland with his tail between his legs. As of right now, this man can no longer do anyone any favors, at least where the court system is concerned. A person who sits on the bench has a lot of power to wield. But now he has been dethroned.

There is also a question lingering about the Kalpoe brothers' history in Surinam. T. J. Ward, a private investigator, told MSNBC's Joe Scarborough, "We have gathered some information right now, and we are trying to verify it, that both of the Kalpoe brothers have been removed from their own country for similar transactions as to what's going on here . . . they may have been taken out of their own country, or asked to leave, and that is why they are living . . . in Aruba. And we are trying to verify this information now and follow up on it."

Two questions come to mind: first, is it possible that one or both of those boys has a problem that he cannot control? And, second, if they did something like this in Surinam, why weren't they prosecuted for it instead of being sent off to live in Aruba? What kind of connections do they have back at home?

I was also able to come up with some interesting information about Joran. While I cannot honestly say what any of it truly means, I am having a hard time considering it totally innocent. At sixteen or eighteen years old, because he listed both ages on the page, he was a member of the MSN network. His member name was "broken_hart_loverboy362." His quote was "Don't hate the player, hate the game!" I may be grasping at straws here, but that seems to be something that comes through loud and clear with this boy. He does not take responsibility for his actions. He feels that he just got into a situation at the wrong place and time, so we should hate the situation that he was in, but not what he himself did. To take it a step further, if the person is caught up in some kind of scheme to hurt girls, it is the scheme that we should dislike, rather than the person. Possibly Joran is letting us know in his own way that there is a much bigger picture involved, like a ring of sex slave traffickers on the island that the boys work for as payback for favors or debts and, remembering his quote, we should hate the traffickers, rather than the boys who do their dirty work. It's all just supposition on my part.

Another question that I have about the boys and the night Natalee disappeared is this: When Joran, Deepak, and Satish left Carlos'n Charlie's with Natalee, Deepak was driving, Satish was in the front passenger seat, and Joran and Natalee were in the back seat. Yet, when the gardener saw the boys in the parked car, he said that Joran was in the driver's seat, Deepak was in the passenger seat, and Satish was in the back seat of the car trying to hide. What could have happened between Carlos'n Charlie's and the area by the Marriott Hotel that would have put them into those different seat positions in the car? After all, according to his mother, Joran didn't even have a driver's license. I doubt whether Deepak would have taken this opportunity, in the middle of the night, to teach Joran how to drive. And, Deepak's mother had commented that he does not allow anyone to drive his car.

Now this is entirely speculative, but I'm trying to work out the possibilities. This is in no way meant to directly implicate anyone involved. But what if Natalee were still in the car with them and they were each taking turns going into the back seat to take advantage of her? Maybe the fact that the gardener saw them influenced them to do "something bad" to her. After all, they may have originally believed that if she managed to get to the police, it would have been her word against theirs and she would be leaving in the morning anyway. She may not have wanted to pursue charges in that situation. But, once the boys had been seen, if Natalee wanted to press charges, their alibis wouldn't work since someone had witnessed them there, so they murder Natalee and ask Paulus to help them get rid of her body. And now the case is significantly more complicated. The boys and whoever else may have been involved with them did not anticipate the way we would handle Natalee's disappearance.

There was only one thing left to do, try to get the gardener off the island right before he was supposed to appear in court.

Another interesting piece of information came from Art Wood, the private investigator who found the gardener. He had made repeated attempts to persuade the gardener to take a polygraph test. When Art first interviewed him, he was convinced that the gardener was sincere and truthful about seeing the three suspects in the field behind the racquet club at 3:00 a.m. on May 30, 2005. Art thought that it would help the gardener's credibility as a witness if he passed a polygraph. However, Eric Mansur, the gardener's employer at the time, seemed to be dead set against him taking the test. In fact, at one point, Eric allegedly threatened to get a restraining order to prevent Mr. Wood from further contact with the gardener. Art advised Eric that a polygraph would help the gardener establish his credibility. Eric said that the police were aware of the gardener and what he had seen in the first week of June, as Eric's sister-in-law was Jan van der Stratten's secretary and she had advised her sister, Eric's wife, of what the gardener had witnessed. Art found it inconceivable that the police could have known about the gardener and not have interviewed him by the end of July.

It is unimaginable when I think about all of the events that transpired over the first few months after Natalee's disappearance, and as I begin to methodically put the pieces together, how an intricate pattern of deceit is so clearly visible. From the tiniest detail to the most significant information, such as the DNA samples that were ruled inadmissible after a judge ordered them to be taken, every single piece of evidence that did exist was disregarded. And everything we did seems to have been a waste of time.

We arrived in Aruba with reinforcements. The authorities sent us to every corner of the island. They had the FBI there for show, and the police held up every phase of the investigation. It seems it was nothing more than a game to them. We thought we were participating in what was happening, but maybe we were just pawns doing their bidding and following their leads. After all, they were the ones who invented the game, and the suspects were the real players. As in Joran's quote, don't hate the players, hate the game. We do, but it isn't over yet.

TEN

Taking the Lead

ON SEPTEMBER 15, 2005, I FLEW BACK TO ARUBA TO follow up on a few more leads and meet once again with the prosecutor, Karin Janssen; the police; and my attorney, Vinda De Sousa. I spent several hours with them and discussed the progress of the case and what I hoped was going to happen next. The police gave the impression that they were just as anxious as I was to solve the case. I received some information from Prosecutor Janssen, but made a promise to her that I would not divulge anything to the public right away because it could damage the case. I also shared with her some of the leads that came in to our e-mail address HelpfindNatalee@comcast.net. Every now and then, some credible tips that warrant further investigation are sent to us. I took the opportunity to follow up on some of them myself, along with my father-in-law, Melvin Parten, who had accompanied me on this trip.

One of the reasons I was in Aruba at that particular time was to do damage control on the island. Apparently, the police were ready to give up on the investigation into Natalee's disappearance because of the boycott against Aruba that Dr. Phil had been advocating. While I was in Aruba, I watched a tape of the show with my lawyer, Vinda De Sousa, and, at the time, I was in complete disagreement with having a boycott. For one thing, I believed that it would interfere with my chances of bringing everyone together in this investigation, including anyone who had tips or leads.

The attorneys and Prosecutor Janssen had requested an uncut version of the tapes that were played on the *Dr. Phil* segment to study for evidence. Those are the tapes that showed the Kalpoes' mother making the statement contradicting her sons' alibis and Deepak making the derogatory statements about Natalee. The prosecutor questioned why Beth did not come to her first with the information that was shown on the tapes, as well as the statement of Natalee's acquaintance who saw her leaving Carlos'n Charlie's on the night she disappeared. I cannot question Beth's motives. We are all unsure of whom to trust. Looking back on everything that has transpired, I wonder what difference it would have made to reveal the information on the tapes to the prosecutor first. Without the world knowing about them before the Aruban investigators, they would have probably been sent off to Holland and never heard about again. Or maybe the authorities would have gone after Jamie Skeeters for trying to get the evidence himself.

In an effort to publicly express my opinion against a boycott, Vinda arranged for me to have an interview with the media. I agreed to do it in the hopes that it would be a good way to show solidarity with the Aruban government.

It is true that we have not been happy with the way the investigation into Natalee's disappearance was going, but we had no gripe with the general population. They have been very hospitable to us throughout this ordeal. Of course, the three boys also had some supporters, but Robin, my family, and I always felt well-received there.

For the most part, the citizens of Aruba are suppressed. I have often wondered if there are Arubans who might know something about Natalee's disappearance, but were remaining silent and going about their business because the Dutch have so much control over everything. Even though there are some Arubans in the system, the Dutch clearly dominate.

I had the opportunity to meet some really wonderful Arubans. Most were sincere and very nice, and it is really sad that a small group of individuals have had such a negative effect on the entire island. That is why I was uncomfortable about supporting a boycott. I did not believe that 100,000 people should be penalized for the actions of a few individuals who are most likely not even from Aruba. I doubt that the regular working-class person had anything to do with Natalee's disappearance, and I felt that their livelihoods should not be penalized with such things as boycotts.

On September 19, 2005, I met with Taylor Northrop. The Aruban government hired him mainly for damage control. He was working with the Strategic Communications Task Force which was comprised of approximately thirteen members of the community, including government spokesperson Rueben Trappenburg, Rob Smith of the Aruba Hospitality & Security Foundation, and other business and political leaders. Taylor thanked me for the press interview I had given denouncing the boycott and advised me that it made his job easier. He said he was hoping that I would be working with everyone rather than promoting a boycott. I gave him some of the information that I had brought along with me, and he was numbed by it. It involved tips that I had received on my Web site.

Taylor is from Fort Lauderdale, Florida, and he was the one who had told me of the prime minister's attempt to have van der Stratten removed from Natalee's case. Taylor also informed me that the reason Jossy Mansur had changed his position about having the FBI brought in was because the case had blown up in the press.

Taylor went on to add that he was involved in the media decisions when Joran, Deepak, and Satish were granted their freedom. It was due to the members of the Strategic Communications Task Force that the media was invited and that their release had taken place during daylight hours to avoid any suspicion. I had to take that bit of information with a grain of salt. The media may have been in Aruba for the suspects' release, but I doubt that their contacts in the United States did not inform them that the number one story was Hurricane Katrina.

Taylor asked if there was anything he could do to return the favor I did by speaking out against the boycott. The following issue immediately came to mind. Tim Miller from Texas Equusearch had contacted me regarding a proposed search of the landfill. A previous attempt to search it had been made; however, the proper equipment was not available. Tim offered to bring in his own equipment and team to Aruba to clear the area. He indicated that the search would not disrupt the flow of refuse to the dump and that any displaced refuse would be returned to its original condition. In other words, what they dug up would be reburied. Also, he assured me that there would be no cost to Aruba for this effort. Tim said he would need the necessary permits to unload a tractor-trailer and the digging equipment at the port in addition to a permit to enter the landfill and any other permits that would be necessary.

I also told Taylor that I needed divers to clear the dock area as well as the necessary permits from the Port Authority. I said I would pay the divers. He contacted me later indicating that there were some divers who were willing to volunteer their services and their time to search the water.

In late September, under the watchful eye of Prosecutor Janssen, the divers went into the waters in the area northwest of the California Lighthouse. They searched through the deep cavern in what most would agree is extremely treacherous water. On the first day, the dive had to be interrupted due to the shift in currents at the underwater cave. The currents were favorable the following day, so the divers were able to get into the cave up to a depth of approximately fifty meters. They could not get in any further, because the rest of the passage was blocked. As with all of the other searches, the dive turned up nothing, but I truly appreciated their efforts. There were arrangements being made for further searches of the marina area and the harbor.

During this time, Prosecutor Janssen told me that she was checking out some very specific leads. She was considering the possibility that Natalee's disappearance was a payback against her uncle, Jar Twitty, Jug's brother. Jar's employer had an international deal that went bad, causing the bank to be fined. Her theory was that people involved in the deal may have been mad at him and took it out on Natalee. I do not really believe that to be the case, especially in light of the fact that Jar's twin sons were in Aruba on the same graduation trip with Natalee and they went home untouched. Prosecutor Janssen was also investigating why the boys did not stay in Aruba when their cousin went missing. This is her investigation and I respect that. I just do not think there is any truth to her suspicions or questions about the twins. Natalee did not have a close relationship with them, but as an independent observer, the prosecutor has to follow through with her leads.

I was also informed that some of Natalee's friends from back home were being questioned by the FBI and that their parents had attorneys present for the questioning. I realize that these kids are wealthy, but I did not understand their need for legal counsel. It has been suggested by Aruban authorities that they are hiding something. My feeling is that the press had pretty much hounded the kids, and there are times when the media does twist some words. The parents probably just wanted to protect their children. I hope they do not believe that we are holding them responsible for what happened to Natalee. We do not fault any of them for this.

Some of the other things that Prosecutor Janssen said she was looking into included the lead that gave her reason to believe that the boys may not have taken Natalee to the beach, as they had claimed.

The police were also looking into Deepak's finances. They felt that a kid with laborer parents and a job in an Internet café should not have such an expensive car with an expensive stereo system in his possession. While I was on that trip to Aruba, I heard that Deepak's stepfather might have purchased the Internet café where Deepak works. The question now is, if that's true, where did they get the money to buy the car and the café? However, Deepak subsequently denied that his stepfather owns the place.

Also, during my meeting with her, Prosecutor Janssen claimed that the FBI never notified the Aruban police about the officers my brother Phil and I saw searching in the sand dunes, which means that the trunk of the police car was never checked for DNA or sand. However, she also stated that she had only heard of this event the day before we met, and she had already summarized it as a presearch to the Dutch Marines coming there. I told her that I felt otherwise, and she suggested that I meet with the detectives and provide them with this information.

I would like to comment about the assertion by Aruban authorities that the FBI had not informed them of various issues in this case. It is something that they have claimed in an effort to explain why they did not follow up on certain leads. I am only stating the things that I have been told and in no way want to denigrate the FBI. I am not saying that I believe the reports from the Aruban government. In fact, I am not sure what to believe anymore. But it is hard to imagine that the FBI would drop the ball on something as important as an American meeting with foul play in a foreign country.

I continue to go out and search in all of the places where tips and evidence lead us. It was on this particular trip in September 2005, that my father-in-law and I searched through the stagnant water at the Bird Sanctuary looking for clues about Natalee. I also attempted to rent a submarine with a glass bottom to search for her. I was hoping to go two miles out to sea, but the Coast Guard said that the submarine was only rated for a shoreline cruise, so I could not use it.

I had to get back home after only about five days on that trip, because the wrath of Hurricane Katrina had left nearly five hundred insurance claims waiting for me on my desk. There was such an overload of work that additional staffing was needed to help me with it so I could not spend as much time in Aruba on that trip as I would have liked.

On Tuesday, September 20, 2005, Melvin and I boarded a jet for home. During our takeoff, we were flying over the island and we noticed there was aggressive digging activity occurring at the landfill in the same area where we had previously conducted a search for Natalee. We saw that a large crane backhoe was digging and piling up garbage at the site. Several large piles had already been dug up. This seemed very unusual, as we had spent a week at the landfill in late July and early August, and the activity of the garbage disposal workers was just the use of bulldozers covering up garbage, rather than digging it up. I was shocked to see the activity there. I notified the authorities in an effort to have them investigate. Apparently, they were just moving things around.

I have made myself more visible to the press in the hopes of receiving more leads. I am also pursuing outside sources to help with our search. I had made contact with someone who has a great deal of experience searching for missing people. In late September 2005, I was introduced through an associate to a man who resides on the West Coast. He had spent twenty-three years in the military and ran an organization that went on rescue missions into foreign countries to find missing children. He was very concerned about our situation. He decided to speak to his associates about coordinating a team to search for Natalee. He sent me an e-mail through my associate. It read:

> In light of the events that have transpired with Natalee Holloway, I write this information and interest statement. If you want more specific information, I can add that later as we get more into the intricacies of the potential mission. In my 23 years of military service and retiring as a Major promotable from the Army, I have had the opportunity to come in contact with special groups who have performed operations out of the ordinary. It is situations such as the Natalee Holloway case where this type of operation might be utilized. I will make some contacts to check on the possibility of a mission to Aruba to attempt a rescue mission or a fact-finding mission for Mr. Holloway. I have had experience with groups working on operations in Venezuela, Colombia and other South American countries. This type of operation is quite difficult and can many times lead to a one-way ticket. The governments on all levels in many of these countries are corrupt, no one is to be trusted, and everyone is suspicious of any outsider. There is a tremendous line of communication amongst the crime groups and any indication of an operation, or for that matter an American looking around for things, spreads like wild fire. Money buys information but you never know if the information is legitimate, is reliable, or a setup until you use it. I make no guarantees for success either stated or implied in this situation. The type of operation this would require is significantly difficult

and obtuse. I am making some inquiries at this time and will contact you with progress in the near future.

I became interested in the fact that the man also told my associate that no front money was desired. I offered him the ability to have the $1,000,000 reward for the safe return of Natalee or we would pay $250,000 for information that helped to solve the case. I received the following e-mail back:

I've been talking with some contacts in the states and in the islands. There are some that are interested but I am in need of more information before I can talk with them in detail and evaluate the situation realistically. I'd like to ask some questions of you, which will help in analyzing the feasibility of the mission. Our goal is a safe and complete extraction and a return of your daughter to the father. Let me state my questions and see what information is available. My concern is time, and what reliable or other information is available and how old it is.

He sent a long list of questions that were necessary in order for him to determine how to go about searching for Natalee or whether a search was even feasible, at that point in time. The questions involved everything from personal information to the climate in Aruba. Then his e-mail continued: "These are a few questions that will assist in getting some idea of what will be needed and to what extent we need to go for any possible extraction if it comes to that. Any additional information you feel would be helpful for planning would also be appreciated."

I answered all of his questions. I knew that he had a picture of what the world already knew, but he needed to hear what only I could supply to him. His reply came to me moments later in an e-mail: "Thank you for providing answers to many of my questions in your case. In light of what you have told me and in doing some more research, I am contacting one of my 'spook' ex-CIA agent friends in the Caribbean to pursue additional intelligence gathering and mission analysis. I'll be in touch."

I was very encouraged by his correspondence, and I hoped that he would be able to bring his team in to help in our search for Natalee. I do not know what has transpired since our correspondence. There are those who pursue various avenues to find Natalee without notifying me of their actions. Some want to do things on the sly to keep their movements covert. Others do not want to be held to following through with something that they may eventually feel is not worthwhile for them or will not bring any results.

Meanwhile, it looked as though other outside entities were also pulling together in an effort to help. Art Wood, who had worked as a volunteer in numerous searches and interviews from early on in the investigation as a guest and investigative advisor of the *Diario* newspaper, sent an e-mail to Prosecutor Janssen with the following information:

Several of the leads we followed leads me to believe that Natalee's body is in the ocean about a mile and a quarter off of the coast from the fishermen's huts. I have located a company in the state of Washington [that] has graciously offered to provide some sophisticated equipment to continue that search. This equipment includes a remote controlled underwater camera which operates in depths of up to 250 feet. The equipment is being shipped directly to Aruba and should arrive within the next week to ten days. The equipment is being shipped to Eduardo Mansur and Eduardo and I will resume the

search once it arrives. We would like the Ar[uban] Police to participate in this search . . .

I did not want to get my hopes up, but I could not help feeling as though the team of experienced searchers, as well as the
equipment that Art was bringing in, could provide us with an
answer. There had to be something that nobody had thought of
in this case. Natalee could not have simply vanished into thin air.
I receive so many tips and leads, and I know that the right one is
waiting to find me. Judging from the e-mails, as well as the message boards and blogs, it is evident that most people really want
to help us. However, every now and then, there are those who
do not seem to be on our side for reasons other than liking Joran
and the Kalpoe brothers. Shortly after the boys' release from
prison, a handful of message boards had comments posted on
them saying that we should get on with our lives and let the
whole investigation go. Some said that the hurricane victims
were more important than one missing girl. However, many
people continued to be supportive. We were grateful for that.
No matter what others think of me, my focus cannot waiver. My
search will not end until I have answers. I have to keep moving
forward to find Natalee.

I felt as though there was a break in the case in early October
2005 when everyone's focus turned to the tapes that Jamie Skeeters
made while he was questioning Deepak Kalpoe about Natalee. It
appeared that Deepak's statement about having sex with Natalee
could have been a turning point in the case, and Dompig acted as
though he was intent upon obtaining the tapes, viewing them, and
sending them to Holland for authentication to see if they had been
altered or edited in any way. I waited anxiously for them to arrive

in Aruba, but as always, there appeared to be red tape holding up their arrival.

One thing I noticed that was not really a focus of the investigation was that Deepak had supposedly told Jamie Skeeters that he believes that Joran murdered Natalee. Skeeters had allegedly asked Deepak if each boy had killed her. "Did you kill Natalee? Did Satish kill Natalee? Did Joran kill Natalee?" Deepak responded, "It wasn't me. It wasn't my brother. So what does that leave?" Skeeters said, "Joran?" Deepak shrugged his shoulders and shook his head indicating yes. Then he agreed to do a polygraph, but he was arrested, so the polygraph never happened. Skeeters said that when he reinterviewed Deepak, he asked him on tape, "Did you kill her?" He answered, "I didn't." Skeeters then asked, "van der Sloot?" He said, "Yes." Deepak also said, "If I knew where the body is I would tell them long time ago. Let them start a trial and get this over with. I don't care."

There it was, a clear statement, and yet there does not seem to be any interest in the fact that Deepak may have accused Joran of murdering Natalee. The focus was only on his comment regarding the three boys having sex with her.

I left for Aruba again early on October 18, 2005. Tim Miller and his searchers came along, as did Art Wood. Beth did not go at that time, because she was told that the Aruban authorities wanted to interrogate her. This made her think that they were considering arresting her. She was also concerned about her safety since she had already received threats, and her attorneys advised her not to return to Aruba yet. But when Aruban authorities asked why she did not travel there on this trip, and she said she was nervous after speaking with her attorneys, she was assured that she would not be arrested if she came back. It all appeared to be a misunderstanding that had hopefully been cleared up.

Shortly after I arrived back in Aruba, I met with Dompig, and he appeared to be acting on his statements. I felt as though we were starting over, which would have been a good thing. He said he was going to go back to the beginning of the case and move forward from there. He directed Tim Miller and me to specific areas to search rather than broad ones. The focus was turning to the sea. I was not sure if his decision was based on new information or not, but Dompig said he had gone through all of the investigative materials and evidence and come to the conclusion that the sea was where we needed to search.

We had recently gotten another tip that the boys did do something to Natalee and that they either left her at the boat launch or the lighthouse. From there, they supposedly went to a field area where the gardener saw them while they planned their next move. According to the tip, after that, they went home and returned the next day to the fishermen's huts to get a steel cage to put Natalee into; they then used a boat to carry her about two to three miles out into the ocean and drop her there. The tip was sent in an e-mail, and we forwarded it to Dompig. He claimed that was one of the reasons to search at sea now instead of at the landfill. In preparation for the search, I met with the Hotel and Tourism Association, the Aruban Tourism Association, and some political leaders and arranged to get some boats and hotel rooms. Thankfully, we were able to get people onto flights, and once they arrived we began the process of searching.

Starting from the area in front of the hotel, we planned to search up to five miles out into the ocean. Using side scan sonar, which means pulling a machine that resembles a torpedo behind the boat at a slow speed to take images up to three hundred feet deep of the bottom of the ocean, we searched for any sign of Natalee. The machine is dragged along at two mph and through a one-hundred-yard path as it maps out the ocean floor and provides a picture on a computer screen similar to radar. We were able to use the machinery for about three days, and then another group came in to take over when I was about to leave. Tim and I made an agreement that if anything were found, I would retain some of the evidence and have it tested for DNA myself.

I had planned to end my trip on Friday, October 21, Natalee's birthday. However, so much activity was going on in Aruba—with the Equusearch team and the equipment that Art Wood had brought in, as well as the tapes arriving—that I did not feel that I could just turn my back and leave. Unfortunately, the sophisticated camera that Art had obtained was not as effective as what Equusearch had with them. But, Equusearch's sonar search capabilities were much better than anything that the Aruban authorities had.

Natalee's birthday was a difficult day. I tried not to focus on it and kept busy with my efforts to search for her. As with times back in Mississippi, I was not always with Natalee on her birthday due to sharing time with her with Beth. I did my best to imagine that this was just not my turn to spend her birthday with her.

During my October trip to the island, another tip came in to my Web site. It was an old post from June 2005 that someone found on a message board and forwarded to me. The details of this latest post were more than interesting. The message had the following information:

Post subject:

Natalee Holloway Questions to be asked of the Two Men

First, I'm very sorry to hear of the very sad case of Natalee Holloway in such a wonderful place like Aruba but it could happen anywhere at any time. There are a few questions that need to be asked of the two men that the FBI are questioning—1st—ask them about the drink that was given to Natalee around 3:15a.m. Aruba time the morning Natalee never returned to her hotel and ask them about the drug in the drink that Natalee drunk without her knowing. 2nd—ask them about the boat and the 2-1/2 mile trip they took. They should break down and tell the truth about the area where Natalee can be found.

Information like that is so specific that I cannot help but wonder who sent it and what else they might know. If they are suggesting questions based on their own knowledge, it is clear they know more. If it is supposition, then it still might be a good guess. So, it was worth investigating.

I have been doing everything I can to keep the search for Natalee alive. My October trip to Aruba originally gave me a small amount of hope because it was the first time I had gotten any guidance from authorities on which areas to search. At the same time, I had to come to some important realizations. Things were happening that made me sit back and reevaluate everything that had transpired and how far we had actually come.

ELEVEN

The "One Happy Island" Conspiracy

DURING MY OCTOBER 2005 TRIP TO ARUBA, WHEN I was not checking my e-mails and messages, I was busy searching. During one of my searches, I heard that the tapes and CD-ROM of Deepak's interview with Skeeters had arrived on the island. However, Dompig commented that he did not think it was a smoking gun. Apparently the transcripts did not match 100 percent what the tapes said. But the tapes were compelling, and Dompig said he was still planning to send them to Holland to have them reviewed for authenticity. If it could be established that there was new information on the tapes that contradicted Deepak's earlier statements, it would help to prove that the three boys were lying. Dompig said that if the tapes were authenticated, it would show a discrepancy to a certain extent, because the boys said they never had sex with Natalee, and the tapes, at the very least, suggested something else.

As far as bringing charges, Dompig said that he did not know yet, because even if the boys had sex with Natalee, he would not know if it was consensual and he did not want to jump to any conclusions about rape. He did say, however, that it might lead to other charges. He wanted to have more answers because there were many issues, e.g., rape, murder, an accident, or people might feel responsible for either knowing too much or taking part in Natalee's disappearance and not want to come forward. So, he was not just looking to find perpetrators. He said he wanted to find the truth.

According to Dompig, there is no crime for lying to authorities in Aruba, but he did say that the lies can give them information about the personality of the person involved, and it could work against that person in front of a judge. He also said that if the tapes were authenticated, Deepak would be brought back to the police station for more questioning.

Dompig saw the tapes of Skeeters's interview with Deepak as having a "stumbling block." He felt that because the transcripts and the tapes did not match exactly, especially where Deepak talked about the boys having sex with Natalee, they needed the experts in Holland to look at the discrepancy. He said that it was unclear whether Deepak had actually agreed with Skeeters or denied it when Skeeters commented, "I'm sure that she had sex with you all." But Dompig did indicate that the fact that Deepak said, "You would be surprised how simple it was" necessitated further investigation.

Dompig also commented about the part of the tape where Deepak can be heard talking, but only the back of his head can be seen. He considered this to be a problem. I do not agree with him. Audiotapes are used as evidence all the time. Voice analysis can be performed to determine if it was really Deepak who was speaking, and the experts would be able to tell if the tapes were edited or altered in any way. The fact that Deepak's face was not shown in part of the interview should not present a problem, in my opinion. I was hopeful that they would make something out of the tapes and find what was necessary to get to the truth about Natalee's disappearance. By that point, it was clear that America knew and everyone else knew what had happened to Natalee, and we just had to prove it.

Frankly, I am getting tired of sitting back and watching things consistently getting twisted to make the smallest details or discrepancies go in the boys' favor. The tapes show that there is a difference between what Deepak has been saying all along and what he said to Skeeters. If the boys did not have sex with Natalee, Deepak would have had no reason to say the words, "You'd be surprised how simple it was." If they did have sex with her, the implication is more than clear. If she resisted or was going in and out of consciousness, then rape seems like the only conclusion. If it was consensual, then where is Natalee? If she agreed to go with them and to have sex with them, then what happened to her that led to her disappearance?

There has been some controversy over this, but we had heard that when the boys made their original statements to police, they said that Natalee was going in and out of consciousness. If they had sex with her under those conditions, Dompig said it would be a felony in Aruba. But the fact that she was passed out and not really aware of what was happening was brought before the judge, and Dompig said he was disappointed because the judge did not accept it. Supposedly the judge did not buy it because Joran went back and forth with his statements, so nothing he said was trustworthy. In my opinion, the fact that he had lied so many times should have been the "smoking gun." Add to that the overwhelming amount of circumstantial evidence in the case, and it should have also been more than enough to bring charges against him. There is only one truth to what happened to Natalee. Innocent people do not have to tell several different versions of events.

That brings me to Joran's father, Paulus. I heard something interesting while I was in Aruba on that trip. Apparently Paulus and Anita van der Sloot had returned there to live. There was a story going around that Paulus was being banned from the court building as long as his son was a suspect. However, we heard a news report that Paulus had petitioned a judge to clear him of any suspicion in connection with Natalee's disappearance. According to the report, he was doing that so he could return to his job with the government. Since his arrest on June 23, 2005, he had been a suspect in the case, and he was seeking an official ruling to change his status and remove him from suspicion. He was supposedly asking for this because he had not been allowed to work since his arrest. However, I heard that not being able to work had not stopped him from receiving his paycheck. The report also stated that since Paulus's contract ended on December 31, 2005, if he did not have his name cleared by then, he could not get his job back. The decision was to be rendered on November 11, 2005. According to what I heard, once his name was cleared, Paulus was planning to file a wrongful arrest suit for $250,000 against the government and get his job back. It seemed to me that he would have wanted that little piece of information to remain confidential until the court's ruling. Considering the way this case has been handled from the beginning, I have no doubt that he will receive a favorable decision from the judge.

It appears that many of the people involved with the investigation into Natalee's disappearance are either corrupt, incompetent, or are pursing an agenda different from finding Natalee. I have been putting the pieces together, and the picture never comes out right. For example, Dennis Jacobs, the lead investigator in the case, is also a narcotics detective. I am wondering why a narcotics cop is investigating a missing persons case. Also, going back to the first day that I arrived in Aruba after Natalee's disappearance, when I found my way to the only police station on the island that had any knowledge that she was missing, the first question that Dennis Jacobs asked me was, "How much money do you have?" I found that to be a curious question to ask the father of a missing teenager. Then, after I informed Jacobs that we were going to start searching for Natalee even if the police weren't, his response was, "Search, why do you want to do that?" When I came back at him with, "Isn't that what you normally do when someone is missing?" His answer was pretty arrogant. He said, "No, this happens all the time. Just go down to Carlos'n Charlie's and have a beer. She'll show up sometime. She probably just got drunk or fell in love and ran off with someone for a few days." Then he advised me that he had taken statements from Joran van der Sloot and Deepak and Satish Kalpoe on the previous day, and he considered them to be compatible in that the boys all said they dropped Natalee off at the Holiday Inn. Even after Beth told him that the tapes at the hotel proved the boys to be lying because they had shown that Natalee did not return there, Jacobs still insisted that Natalee would probably show up soon. The worst part of that was the fact that Jacobs was already aware that the tapes proved the boys to be lying when he told me that their stories were compatible. My brother and I insisted that Jacobs question the boys again, and it took him several days to do that.

Also, we have been shown some of the statements taken in the case and, from what we have seen, there were answers that Jacobs should have definitely followed up on. For example, Joran said, "I think that Deepak killed Natalee and buried her body." Jacobs asked nothing regarding how he did it, why he did it, or where it happened. However, Jacobs had no problem when it came to interrogating Natalee's family members. He questioned me extensively during my October trip. The main reason he was meeting with me had to do with what Paulus van der Sloot and I had talked about at the prison when I went there in an attempt to see Joran in August 2005. Jacobs and I talked for over an hour and a half about that discussion, and he questioned me about various things, including a statement Paulus had made insinuating that a Mountain Brook student needed to be investigated. He also wanted to know if I gave Natalee $500 for her graduation gift. He asked me that because Joran maintained that it was Natalee who lost the money at the casino, not her friend as we had been told, and that he had won part of it back for her. Jacobs implied that I would have been angry with Natalee for losing the money I gave her at a casino. However, Natalee had deposited that money into her bank account the day after I gave it to her, and she did not bring it with her on the trip. And, if she had brought it and lost it, what difference would that have made in the investigation? It was her money to use however she wished. I would not expect her to gamble it away. But, if she had, she would have been wise enough on her own to learn an important lesson from that. She would never have even considered running away. This is a young woman who had everything anyone could dream of right within her reach, and a little overindulgence on her graduation trip would not have influenced her to throw it all away.

Jacobs also asked me if Beth is related to Hitler. What a ridiculous question! I told him that, to my knowledge, Beth is not related to anyone in Germany. Apparently, Joran claimed that Natalee had made a comment about Beth while she was in the car with the boys. I am not too sure about it, but I gathered it had something to do with Natalee being asked how strict her mother is and answering jokingly that she was related to Hitler or something to that effect. For anyone to take that literally is beyond me. They are looking at the most nonsensical things to take the attention away from the real issues and the most logical suspects.

I could not believe my ears when Jacobs asked me the next question. He wanted to know how much money Beth and I each have. I sat there in disbelief. I was astounded. There we were, five months after my daughter went missing, and he was asking me the same question that he asked the very first time we met. I could not help but wonder what difference it made, then or now. I thought for a moment and then responded, "Enough to spend the next forty years on this case." I hope I made my point. However, looking back at that moment, I now reflect on a much different response, "Enough to keep my promise to Natalee. We will never give up on her."

All of the above questions had been asked and answered during my prior trips to Aruba. Communication between the departments as well as with us, or the lack thereof, was the main reason I was there in Aruba on that trip. And there we were, going in circles once again.

Next, I had to listen to Jacobs's theories as to what happened to Natalee. He surmised that she is either alive and ran away because she was unhappy with Beth and she is too embarrassed to come home until things calm down; or that Beth orchestrated this whole ordeal to make money; or that Joran took Natalee to the beach, got her drunk, left her there, and the Mountain Brook boys raped her, then took her out on a boat and killed her; or that the three suspects drugged her, killed her, took her out on Joran's friend Koen's boat in a cage, and dumped her into the sea. I cannot help but wonder if Jacobs has been receiving tips on the Internet. I read all of the same theories every single day on my Web site. I would have hoped that he could have come up with something more substantial than that by now.

While I was there on that trip, I heard that Dompig was investigating Koen. He supposedly writes Joran every day. I had read

Joran's deposition and knew Koen to be his best friend, and when I was on the island at an earlier time, some teenagers had told me it was Koen's boat that took Natalee out to sea. Art Wood and I drove by Koen's house and saw a boat around the side, and Koen and his father were out there working on it. The front door was wide open, and we decided to drive by a few times. One time, Koen was walking into the living room, and he saw us going by slowly, so he barrel-rolled and hid behind the couch. I wondered what must have been going through his mind to make him hide like that. We later learned that Koen's mother had told someone that when Freddy was arrested, Koen was so scared that he slept in his parents' bed with them on at least one occasion.

After Dompig heard that we had found the boat, he indicated that he was going to bring Koen in for questioning in a day or so. I told him that if they interviewed Koen, they might solve the case. Since we were investigating Koen and his boat, Art and I decided to drive down to the beach to see where the boats are launched into the ocean. We went back to about halfway between the Marriott Hotel and the fishermen's huts, and while we were looking around, we saw a cross about a foot and a half high with the initials "N.H." carved into the wood and a rosary hanging from it. I was really taken by surprise. It was the first time that it hit me so hard, the thought of Natalee being dead. The cross was obviously a memorial to her, and I was not ready to accept that we needed anything like that yet. I was still holding out some hope for finding her alive, and coming face-to-face with the cross was like a punch in the stomach.

Art and I did not believe that it was put there by accident. If someone was just putting something out in memory of Natalee and they did not know anything about what had really happened to her, they would have probably put it at the California Lighthouse or the fishermen's huts. We wanted to find out who might be involved in Natalee's case that might be a Catholic. A man who puts boats in the water every day at the site said the cross suddenly appeared about a month to a month and a half before. We immediately called Dompig and informed him about it. He said he would have Jacobs call us.

Later that afternoon, Art and I went to a Catholic Church to speak with the priest to see if he could tell us anything. We talked to his secretary, and she told us that the priest was in mass and we should come back the next day. We made an appointment to come back, and the following afternoon, while we were eating, a group from *America's Most Wanted* came and interviewed us. Art and I were about to leave to meet with the priest when we received a phone call from Dompig saying that he had been contacted by the priest asking about why we wanted to meet with him. After that, the priest said he would not be available for the next three days. I would be gone by then. I did not think that to be a coincidence.

On one of the last days of my trip, I met Dompig in a parking lot, and he asked me about a bone that a tourist had recently found. I didn't know anything about it at the time. Jacobs called me to say he had heard reports from the United States that a bone had been found on the beach in Aruba. He had assumed that the reports had come from me. He yelled at me, asking what I was doing releasing the information and told me that all the evidence has to go through him. I had begun to realize that any evidence that went through Jacobs never seemed to make its way to Holland. It was either disregarded or it disappeared. I mentioned the cross to Jacobs, and he did not think anything of it. We just wanted to know why it was placed where it was. Then, Dompig told us that we were stepping over the line. So we dropped the cross story.

Later, I heard that a tourist found a bone and gave it to the beach police, but they supposedly did not feel comfortable about giving it to Dompig, so they passed it along to someone over his head. The last I heard was that they felt the bone had been in the water for too long and therefore it was probably not related to Natalee. It appears to be just another piece of potential evidence that was swept under the rug without any forensic testing.

Not long after that, I received a communication from a woman who said that she was the one who had put the cross up. This was what she told me:

I own a Marriott time-share on Aruba and I walk that part of the beach every morning. The very first time I walked past the fishing huts, I had to stop. I had this awful feeling that something bad could happen there and nobody would know.

When Natalee disappeared, I listened to the news and thought that this is the same part of the beach I walk and get these strong feelings that something bad could happen there.

On my trip to Aruba in October, I had to look around the fishing huts. On my morning walks, I poked around in the sand. I found nothing but felt I had to do something for Natalee. . . . The next morning on my walk, I took the cross and with a rock, I pounded it into the sand on the mound, put some rocks around the bottom and wrapped my rosary beads around it. I thought, God will watch over you every day now, no matter where you are, AND you will not be forgotten.

I left the next morning. On the way to the airport, I asked the cab driver if he thought the Holloway case would ever be solved. His answer was, "No, because there was no body." He went on to tell me he once worked for the Aruban Police Department and that he was 99.9% sure the father knew something and that he was involved. I got the impression that the locals do not like the van der Sloots.

The cab driver referred to the father as "That Dutchman." I told him
I feel there is a dark cloud hanging over the island and it will remain
until the truth comes out.

We are looking for the cab driver to see if he can tell us anything about the case. The cross may not have brought us anything
significant about Natalee, but maybe the cab driver will. We
never know what may lead us to the answer.

While still in Aruba, I found out that there was a prosecutor
named Amalin Flanegan who had resigned from Natalee's case
about a month into it. She had worked along with Karin Janssen,
and she had to report to Theresa Croes Fernandez-Pedra, the
attorney general. I wanted to know why she had resigned. Art and
I met with Ms. Flanegan at a local restaurant, and she seemed very
apprehensive. We told her how we felt about the way the investigation was going, how the evidence had been dealt with, Dennis
Jacobs's handling of the interviews, and that there were important
things missing. We explained how we were first told that there was
blood in Deepak's car. Then, there was no blood in the car. The seat
had been cut out of the car, and it tested positive for blood. Then,
it supposedly tested positive for chocolate syrup and cleaning
fluid. But the prime minister had said that it was definitely blood,
and a police officer that Art talked to said it tested positive for
blood. Art also told Ms. Flanegan about how the police disregarded the evidence of the belt that was found that was similar to
the one Joran had used on his Web site and the pieces of plastic discovered near the same area. I was also reminded of the fact that I
had never heard anything more about testing being done on any of
the bones that had been found—more evidence that was ignored or
dismissed as irrelevant. I could not help but recall the donkey and
fish bones that were discovered early in July 2005. A tourist had

found one of them near the California Lighthouse, and it still had the flesh intact. It resembled a shoulder bone and the tourist turned it in to the Noord Police and contacted me about it. The police had never informed me of the find. When I inquired about the bone, Dennis Jacobs informed me that a donkey bone and a fish bone had been found. Another investigator from the team said that a human bone was found, but that it was too old to have belonged to Natalee. I assumed that it had been sent for forensics testing. But I really have no idea what happened to it, if it was tested, discarded, or even investigated in any way.

I suddenly realized that Dennis Jacobs seemed to have a hand in so many things that were unexplainable. I thought about Jacobs asking me how much money I have and the statements the boys gave with no follow-up questions. Then, I recalled how an FBI agent had told Beth that when Dennis was conducting interviews, she became so frustrated that she had walked out, because it seemed as though he did not want to do the interrogation. She said there were no follow-up questions asked regarding important issues that were being raised so I was right about that. She felt the questioning had not been handled properly, and it was not just my own opinion.

I also had to give some serious thought to Karin Janssen, the prosecutor. She has been in charge of the prosecution on Natalee's case and, to date, not one of her efforts have been successful.

Art and I talked to Ms. Flanegan about all of the red flags that we were seeing and that we thought that Koen, Joran, and Deepak took Natalee out in the boat. She agreed with that theory. She added that the reason she had left the case was because she thought Koen was lying, and when she asked the police to reinterview him, they refused. We told her that we were going to talk to the prime minister the next day to lay it all out.

I then contacted Dompig to talk to him about my thoughts on Dennis Jacobs, but he was very supportive of him. I asked Dompig to do the interview of Koen instead of having Jacobs do it. I became concerned because he said he would have to discuss it with Jacobs first. Several weeks later, I heard that Koen's father had been interviewed, but Koen had not been questioned yet. I wondered if they were prepping the father to prep his son for questioning. That was something that seemed all too familiar.

The day after our talk with Ms. Flanegan, I had to go to the police station to turn in the statement that I had given to Dennis Jacobs. He had given me a copy to go over with my attorney, Vinda. But, after looking at it, I realized that it was only a page and a half long and had little to do with what we had actually discussed the most, the conversation that I had with Paulus van der Sloot at the prison. Instead, it focused on three other questions: the one about the $500 gift to Natalee, the one about Beth being related to Hitler, and the fact that Paulus had pointed to a Mountain Brook student he said needed to be investigated, a statement he had obviously made to divert attention away from the three boys. That was it. I had spent a long time with Jacobs, and much of my interview was not in the statement.

When I went back to turn it in and discuss it with him, I was told that Jacobs was in with Jan van der Stratten. Later, I went back again and Charles Croes was sitting there with Jacobs. He is the guy who gets cell phones for tourists on the island. I wondered if he was there to report to Jacobs about the phones he rents out. What else would the cell phone guy be doing sitting with the lead detective? He mentioned to me how dignified I have been through this whole investigation. I think he was trying to distract me from the fact that I found him in there, because I have reason to believe that the cell phones we use on the island are being monitored. As mentioned previously, even the press sometimes seemed to be one step ahead of me as when they thought I was going to identify a body. And, when I first arrived on the island, an attorney told me that the cell phones there are non-secure and can be monitored. I commented to Jacobs about how short my statement was. He said that I could add anything I wanted to it. Also, I noticed that Eric Soemers's name was on it, but that detective was not even present during the interview. Now I wondered if Jacobs was making up everyone's statements and getting Eric to sign onto them. If that were the case, he could state anything he wanted, and it would look like an official statement made in front of a witness.

I asked Jacobs to print me out another copy of my statement, and Art Wood came walking in. He noticed a computer printout on the wall about Natalee's case. It was a flowchart with all of the suspects and interested parties on it. He noticed that one person who we thought was a suspect, Lorenzo van Rijn, rumored to be Joran's half brother, was not on it. We had been told that he might have had some connection to Natalee's disappearance. He is supposedly known on the island by the nickname Xtacy. Art was trying to figure out how the flowchart worked, and he noticed that some of the names were significantly larger than others. He asked Jacobs what that symbolized, and Jacobs responded that it was just the way the computer printed it out. Art asked him where Lorenzo was, and Jacobs said that Lorenzo had nothing to do with Natalee's case, so he doesn't have to be on the flowchart. We left, and Art commented on Jacobs's reaction. There is talk in Aruba that Lorenzo is a known drug dealer who lives in a compound on the island with a remote-controlled sliding gate, television monitors, and razor wire all around the top of the fence. Apparently, you cannot get into that place. It looks like a prison camp. Since Lorenzo is supposed to be related to Joran, if the boys got drugs to give Natalee, they may have gotten them from him. There was also speculation that he has something to do with the rave houses that are discussed in the "Shango" appendix.

On that trip, I also met with Satish's attorney. All he had to say was that the boys dropped Natalee at the beach, and they are all innocent. I cannot imagine him saying anything other than that about his client. He is going to say whatever he can to maintain his client's innocence. However, I have come to believe that he is not the only one who is saying whatever he can to take the focus off of the three boys.

Dompig began talking out of both sides of his mouth. On October 26, 2005, he made a comment to the Aruban press that shocked me. He was quoted in a local newspaper calling for an investigation into the millions of dollars Beth Twitty has received through the Natalee Holloway fund. His theory about the case is that Beth has millions and maybe she is responsible for Natalee's disappearance. He indicated that Beth had planned to raise money and make millions off of Natalee's disappearance and that she is still alive somewhere. If Dompig believed that to be the case, why was he even wasting everyone's time with his reassurances that he was going to start the investigation over from square one? Was that just another diversion to keep us from making more waves? It is disgraceful that he has turned his teams' bungling of the investigation into an attack on Natalee's parents for doing everything we can to find her. To our faces he promises diligence, and behind our backs he promotes anti-Holloway-Twitty sentiment. He had to know we would find out. What message was he really trying to convey to us? Maybe he thought we would start attacking each other and stop focusing on the Aruban government. Divide and conquer! Instead, we circled the wagons and planned our next move.

TWELVE

Shaking Up the Hornet's Nest

WHILE STILL ON MY OCTOBER TRIP TO ARUBA, ART accompanied me to see Beth's attorney, Helen Lejuez. She informed us that Jan van der Stratten had been responsible for a previous cover-up on the island. She also said that she felt her cell phone was being monitored. I let her know that I had been feeling the same way. I wondered what had happened to the three girls who came forward claiming that Joran had raped them. Helen said they had dropped their cases. She knew one of them, so she called the girl to find out why. The girl was going to come in to talk to Art the next day and tell him why she did not go forward with her case, but she cancelled her appointment. We later learned that it was after she had talked to Dennis Jacobs that she decided to drop her case.

While at Helen's office, we met with a man named Roland Peterson, a former high-ranking official within the police and immigration departments. He has been retired for several years, and he writes children's books on the island. He said he was aligned to help us out regarding evidence on corruption.

Helen also set up a meeting for us with Prime Minister Oduber, so we jumped into her secretary's car and were immediately driven to the meeting. The prime minister had given instructions that this was to be a "courtesy" meeting with no press. He wanted it to be a quick chat, and we were to come and go unseen. We pulled up to the front of the building and rushed inside. We met with the prime minister and his assistant. We felt it necessary to tell him that we had seen Jan van der Stratten in Dennis Jacobs's office. He seemed quite surprised and blew up at that. He said van der Stratten was not even supposed to be inside the police station.

We informed him that it was our feeling that every phase of the investigation had been mishandled and jeopardized by the current investigative and prosecution team. We expressed to him our total lack of confidence in the team and made a very strong request that a new one be assigned to continue with the investigation into Natalee's disappearance. He stated that he could not consider our concerns unless we put them in writing. The meeting ended, and we left just as quickly as we had arrived, trying not to be seen. The prime minister did not want any publicity. It was supposed to be a secret meeting. Some secret! The morning after I returned home, I got a call from my attorney's assistant asking me about the meeting. She had gotten a call from a reporter saying that we were at the prime minister's office with Beth's attorney. She wanted to know what was going on. I explained that it was just a courtesy visit.

I also received a call from Tim Miller telling me that Dompig did not want to cooperate with us anymore. Tim had met with the FBI the day before about the equipment we needed to continue the ocean search. Due to the depth of the waters and the distance of three to five miles into the ocean that we needed to go, our search had exceeded the capability of the equipment that was currently in use. Tim had to ask Dompig for a letter of approval to use the FBI equipment, and Dompig told him that he did not have time. I am not sure what the stonewalling was about. I suppose it had something to do with our request to have everyone removed from the case. There are plenty of other detectives that would be more qualified to handle Natalee's case, and in light of what I had learned while on this that trip, it seemed more than prudent to put Amalin Flanegan back on it.

Tim also informed me that neither the Aruban police department nor the prosecutor's office had made the request for FBI assistance with a dive team yet. I had provided an e-mail with all of the contact information that was necessary in order to proceed forward in concluding the search and hopefully bring the investigation to an end. It appeared our search efforts could not proceed until this communication issue was resolved. Permission had to be granted. I didn't understand what had happened. In my first meeting with Dompig during my October trip, he made it clear that he needed the FBI's help. But by the time they showed up, things had gotten quiet.

Further, Dompig made statements to the media about the Deepak tapes to the effect that there was a large backlog of information that needed to be analyzed, and everything in the Dutch Kingdom has to be handled by only one lab, so the tapes were not a top priority. He said that the Dutch authorities had other things going on, and the tapes could only be analyzed in the order in which they were received. At that point, Natalee had been missing for five months, and Dompig was implying that something that came into the lab a week before would be analyzed before the evidence in her case. It was apparently just another stalling tactic.

I knew things had changed while I was in Aruba during that trip, but I did not think it would become so obvious to the general public. I had not supported the idea of a boycott because I did not want to hurt the people of Aruba. The governor of Alabama, Bob Riley, wanted me to go along with him on it, but

I told him that I would not and I had him call Prime Minister Oduber to tell him that. I still felt that a lot of people who had nothing to do with the case would suffer from a boycott. I did not want to hurt the poor people, but I began to feel that Aruba needed to step up to the plate and take some immediate action in order to prevent one. If the Aruban government continued to make such blatant statements about putting Natalee's case on the back burner, I could not be responsible for what others in the United States would do.

Tourism, which, according to Aruba.com is the "main pillar of the Aruban economy," was already suffering. On my second or third day there during my October trip, the Aruban Tourism Association wanted me to meet with the local press to give them a statement. I arrived there and they were busy, so I had to wait. I noticed a gentleman angrily walking out. He was complaining to a lady that she must have changed the picture of his hotel on the Aruban Web site because he had been getting about seven hundred hits a day and now he was getting only forty. He commented, "I'm going to be out of business. You need to change it back to what it was a couple of months ago." I had good reason to believe that his loss of hits did not have anything to do with someone changing the picture of his hotel. Later, I had to go to the Holiday Inn to buy phone minutes, and while I was talking to the cashier, a lady came in and overheard me and said, "You sound just like Dave Holloway." She said, "Come here," and we walked out into the lobby. She told me that she was thinking of selling her timeshare because the whole situation surrounding Natalee's disappearance had opened her eyes. She traveled to Aruba every couple of months, and she said there was more crime there than she had originally thought. She told me that she had been shopping downtown and noticed how empty it was.

She looked around and commented, "Where is everybody?" She was told that it was the off-season. She said she asked if the lack of tourists was really about the Natalee Holloway case and the response she got was, "I can guarantee you get more crime in the United States than here." She said, "What about the three boys?" And they said, "What about O. J.?" She became annoyed and said, "To hell with you!" She told me she did not like the way they were talking about Natalee, so she didn't pay for her things. She just walked out and left them there. I told her, "Good for you!" I am sure that she is not the only tourist who is fed up with what has happened regarding Natalee's investigation.

As I was getting on the plane to leave, I felt as though I had thrown a rock at a hornet's nest. The main purpose of my trip was to make everyone aware of what I felt was really going on with the investigation and to force changes to be made. I knew there would be a shake-up down there very soon. I had become more outspoken. I had originally focused more on searching than doing interviews with the press. But I had also felt that the Aruban investigators were working with us to find Natalee. All that has changed. I am now doing my best to see that the truth comes out and to make sure that a qualified team is put together in Aruba to continue with the investigation.

On November 1, 2005, Art Wood, Beth and Jug Twitty, and Robin and I put together a six-page document stating the concerns that Art and I had expressed to Prime Minister Oduber in Aruba. We sent it to Theresa Croes Fernandez-Pedra, attorney general of Aruba, with copies forwarded to Prime Minister Oduber; Rudy Croes, the Aruban minister of justice; Helen Lejuez, Beth's attorney; Vinda De Sousa, my attorney; Bob Riley, the governor of Alabama; and Condoleezza Rice, the United States secretary of state. Our hope was that a new team would be put in place, one that would investigate Natalee's disappearance with the integrity and thoroughness that she deserves.

Then, something quite unexpected happened here in the United States. On November 2, 2005, Dr. Phil went on *The Tonight Show* and stated, "Without creating false hope, we have reasonable belief and some credible evidence that Natalee Holloway is alive." He discussed the sex slave industry and suggested that it is the main focus of the investigation. I was concerned that his public announcement might have elicited the wrong reaction. If there is any chance that Natalee is alive and being held captive as a sex slave, the fact that Dr. Phil announced that as a focal point of the investigation might encourage those holding her to take her into an even more remote location than where she may already be. In the event that she is not alive, he has given an incredible sense of false hope to those people who have remained steadfast with their support and prayers for us.

I assume that the credible evidence that Dr. Phil referred to had something to do with information that we had been keeping confidential. On Monday, October 3, 2005, Beth's private cell phone received a voice mail message. When Beth went to retrieve it, she heard the voice of a girl calling, "Mom, help me." She was able to hear other voices in the background. She reported the call to the FBI, and they were going to do a voice analysis to compare it to the audios we have of Natalee and also attempt to determine from where the call originated.

I do not want to get my hopes up. I have tried to cling to some hope that Natalee will come back to us. I am afraid to do that again. There have been so many ups and downs. I have to wait this one out and pray for some good news.

There was some other interesting information that surfaced about Natalee. A *Diario* reporter said that he had been tracking her since the beginning of the investigation and that he saw her being moved from one house to another in Aruba on three separate occasions in June, July, and August 2005. He said that her hair had been dyed, but he felt sure it was Natalee. He claimed that every time he was getting close to going in and rescuing her, the authorities, who he said must have been tipped off that he was getting close, would move in and ruin his plans. He said that he was setting up rescues and, at one point, he followed a silver car that was carrying Natalee and when it reached a certain house, a helicopter flew in and picked up the people who had gotten out of the car. I doubt his story is credible. I don't think he was lying, but I do feel that he was mistaken. However, I do not completely discount it, especially in light of all of the different stories that we have heard about the night Natalee disappeared. Considering all that I have learned about the "One Happy Island" of Aruba, I cannot ignore the possibility that she was there, right under everybody's noses while we were scouring the beaches for her. In fact, the main suspects in the case had more than enough time and influence to turn this entire ordeal into a game of cat and mouse. Isn't that what Shango was trying to tell us in the riddles? (See appendix.) It was all happening right out in the open. The Arubans and the Dutch knew what had happened to Natalee. The signs were all there, but the Americans were being deceived with lies.

I have been told that Dr. Phil's people have been sweeping the islands looking for Natalee. I am truly grateful to him for that, and I am hopeful that they will be successful. And, even if they do not find her, perhaps they will uncover the whereabouts of someone else, like Amy Bradley, or another person being held captive in one of those sex slave houses.

The morning after Dr. Phil's announcement, a woman who was in Aruba when Natalee disappeared contacted me. She said that on the night that Natalee went missing, she had seen two men dressed in suits who did not appear to be tourists, trying to coerce a pretty young woman to go with them. This happened across the street from the Holiday Inn where Natalee was staying. The woman had the impression that they had something to do with royalty. That seemed significant since there was supposedly a Saudi prince whose boat was docked in Aruba while Natalee was there. The woman continued, saying that she did not connect it to Natalee's disappearance at the time, and then she left the island and was away for over a month and did not follow news reports. But, when she heard Dr. Phil on *The Tonight Show,* she remembered what she had seen and decided that she had to look me up to tell me about it. So, Dr. Phil's publicity stirred someone's memory about the night that Natalee disappeared. We never know who is out there who has not kept up with our story and who might have some relevant information that they have yet to come forward with.

While Dr. Phil's comments on *The Tonight Show* may have produced some mixed results, there is no question about what his actions in total have had in Aruba. Shortly after his appearance, Aruban officials released the following statement:

> At this time the investigative team, which consists of police agents from the Aruban Police Force under guidance of the prosecutor in charge of this case, is at work in several areas of the criminal investigation into the disappearance of Holloway last May of this year. In the first place the team is busy investigating aspects and leads that have not been investigated yet.
>
> The investigative team is also interviewing new witnesses and witnesses who have already been interviewed in this case are being interviewed again. Yesterday for instance, members of the police

team interviewed the mother of the missing Miss Holloway. She was on the island for a couple of days.

Besides investigating new leads or leads that have not been investigated yet and interviewing new witnesses and witnesses who have already been interviewed the team is reviewing the whole investigation from the start until now. From this review the team has concluded that there are several aspects that need more attention, for instance there are people living in the United States of America who have to be interviewed again, this time more profoundly. To realize this, the Public Prosecutor's Office has petitioned the United States of America for legal assistance. When there is more information about this request that can be made public, the Public Prosecutor's Office will make this information public.

The last development that will be highlighted in this press release regards the tapes of the Dr. Phil show. During this show a couple of weeks ago a tape was shown in which one suspect in the case of the disappearance of Miss Holloway makes declarations about the case on camera to a private investigator. After requesting and receiving these tapes from the United States of America the tapes were sent to the Dutch Forensic Institute in Holland for further testing. The results of these tests are not known yet.

The Public Prosecutor's Office will keep on working as it always has, which is according to the law.

It is not surprising that the statement focused on Natalee's mother, Beth, as well as "people from the United States" who need to be questioned again. They say that this time they will do it "more profoundly." There is an obvious omission. They fail to mention the three main suspects, the boys who were the last people to be seen with Natalee, who have told so many different and conflicting versions of their night with her. The impression the statement gives is that the investigative team is diligently pursuing the truth in Natalee's case when, in fact, it appears that they have actually done just about everything they can to divert attention away from those who should be scrutinized the most. Hopefully, they will see the error of their ways and reinterview the people most likely responsible for Natalee's disappearance as "profoundly" as they plan to question the innocent American tourists.

Our demand for a new team of investigators received a response that was directed to Bob Riley, the governor of Alabama. The Department of Foreign Affairs in Aruba basically let us know that the commissioner of police was appointed by the Dutch government, and that the chief prosecutor leading the investigation and the general prosecutor are appointed by the Kingdom Government in the Hague; therefore, because of the separation of powers, the government of Aruba has no authority to intervene in the investigation, and the attorney general stated that she did not have the authority to dismiss the current investigative teams—only the Hague could do that. We were shocked. In all these months and with all of our direct dealings with investigators, prosecutors, and government officials, we had never once been directed to the Hague to seek help. All this time we had been led to believe that those individuals with the complete authority to conduct and supervise the investigation into Natalee's disappearance were already working on her case. Now, after all this time and all of our efforts, we have come to the realization that we have been going in circles.

On November 8, 2005, Alabama Governor Bob Riley held a televised press conference with Beth and Jug Twitty at his side during which he called for a travel boycott of Aruba. He also urged all fifty states to back him in the boycott, stating, "Until their lack of law enforcement practices can be evaluated, and until they offer some resolution in Natalee's case, tourists are not safe in Aruba or any Dutch territories."

In response to Governor Riley's call for a boycott, Aruban officials complained to the U.S. Department of State asking them to put a stop to it. Prime Minister Oduber called the boycott a "preposterous and irresponsible act" and told reporters that "Aruban investigators have done their best to solve the mystery and the entire island doesn't deserve to be punished . . ."

While I still had mixed feelings about a boycott, I stood strong in supporting my government in any decisions they made. The people of Aruba have elected their officials, and their officials have spoken. We elect our officials, and they have decided what is necessary for the people.

On November 11, 2005, in the midst of the threat of a boycott looming over Aruba, an Aruban court issued a decision releasing Paulus van der Sloot from any suspicion in Natalee's case. In spite of the fact that the prosecutor had accused him of obstructing the investigation by telling Joran, Deepak, and Satish, "When there is no body, you don't have a case" and sending for one of Joran's friends to find out what he had told police when he was questioned; in spite of changing his story about the night of Natalee's disappearance when he first said he picked Joran up at 4:00 a.m. and then switching it to 11:00 p.m. when he realized his son needed an alibi; in spite of giving statements to the press that conflicted with what he had already told police during questioning; in spite of the prime minister assuring me that "Nobody is above the law"; in spite of Paulus's June 23, 2005, arrest on "suspicion of complicity to premeditated murder, complicity to kidnapping and murder and kidnapping"; in spite of Dompig's son telling me that he had heard that Paulus had borrowed a friend's boat on either the night of Natalee's disappearance or the next day and that he was involved with Natalee's murder; and in spite of Paulus's statement to me that "As the father of Joran, I will do everything to protect my son," he has been officially declared free and clear of having any involvement in Natalee's disappearance. In my view, this was just another strike against the investigative team that told me that we needed their immediate removal. Ironically, Paulus had the audacity to announce plans to file a wrongful arrest suit against the government. As if that was not enough, apparently, on Friday, December 9, 2005, Steve Cohen, the new spokesperson for the Strategic Communications Task Force for Aruba, discussed on MSNBC's *Rita Cosby Show* a letter that Paulus van der Sloot claimed that he received from Natalee. The letter supposedly contained an explanation from Natalee as to why she ran away from Beth and says that she is living in the United States. She also tells the Dutch authorities that to verify that the letter is really from her, they should test it for her DNA. Paulus has allegedly turned the letter over to Dompig who, in turn, has sent it to the Netherlands for forensic testing. My response to that information is that if there is a letter with Natalee's DNA on it, someone did something to her and put her DNA on the letter to try to cover up a crime, and the authorities should look to the person who had possession of that letter and investigate him first and foremost.

Considering all that had transpired, I changed my position. In early December 2005, I called Mississippi Governor Haley Barbour's office to ask that he join Alabama Governor Bob Riley and Arkansas Governor Mike Huckabee in the travel boycott of Aruba. Since that time, Georgia Governor Sonny Purdue has also come on board in support of the boycott. However, I had waited over a month to hear back from Governor Barbour when he made an announcement that he will not join in on the boycott. I am surprised that he never responded to me, and I am truly disappointed that he does not feel a boycott is warranted.

I can no longer sit on the fence on this issue. It has not been an easy decision for me to make. But I need to know what happened to my daughter, and I do believe that a boycott may be the only way we will get anybody over there to talk to us or to turn in the people who are responsible for her disappearance.

Back on December 12, 2005, Jossy Mansur had reported on Fox News that Karin Janssen, chief prosecutor in Natalee's case, was to be fired on December 16, 2005. It was also reported that the police have threatened to quit the case if a new prosecutor who is supposedly coming in from Curacao takes over. We thought that the changing of the guard had begun. We have since been informed that Karin Janssen is still on Natalee's case and working hard to find answers for us. We are grateful for that. However, in December 2005, Aruban officials also told us that Natalee's case would be closed in sixty days. I cannot let that happen!

Due to the many inconsistencies and the threat that the door is being closed on Natalee's investigation, I do not feel comfortable leaving the entire investigation in the hands of the authorities in Aruba. There are too many things happening there that concern me. We were informed that the three main suspects, Joran van der Sloot, and Deepak and Satish Kalpoe, would be brought in and requestioned while Joran was back in Aruba for his Christmas break from college. But his stay there came and went without the interrogation that had been publicly promised. In fact, Karin Janssen stated that since the court had released the boys with prejudice, they cannot be ordered to come in for questioning. They can only do it voluntarily. We were not made aware of that when the promise to bring them back in was made.

So, rather than waiting around to find things out secondhand, with the help of those who have been working alongside me, I have continued with my own investigation. I thought I had tried everything I could conceivably imagine to find the answers that would resolve this tragic mystery, but nothing positive had materialized. As a last resort, Larry Garrison, who, as mentioned earlier is an executive producer in film and television, collaborated with me in an attempt to get two of the boys to speak out. We had heard that Deepak Kalpoe was interested in making a book deal. He thought his story would bring him a lot of money. Right before Christmas, Larry contacted Deepak at the Internet café where he works. He proposed the possibility of doing a book and film with Deepak and his brother Satish. Larry and Deepak began conversing on the phone and sending e-mails via the Internet. I checked Deepak's Internet address and concluded that it was his and that he was writing from three locations within Aruba. We knew that there were other people on the Internet who were posing as Joran and Deepak, so we had to make sure we were actually dealing with Deepak. Finally, Larry was able to get Deepak's private cell phone number. He also continued to speak to him at his business. Larry attempted to convince Deepak to tell his story and talk about what happened to Natalee, but Deepak was only interested in talking about himself. At one point, Deepak wrote Larry an e-mail saying that it was his story, and nobody gave a damn about Natalee Holloway. I thought it funny that Deepak could envision anyone wanting to buy a book about his life without any information about his connection to Natalee.

Larry offered to have Deepak and his brother fly to the United States under the premise of trying to set up a film and book deal. He was even able to get a publisher who sympathized with our plight to agree to set up a meeting with Deepak and Satish. Larry planned to film it in the hopes that if they said something incriminating, we could use it as evidence. We wanted to have someone from the FBI there, but we were told that if we were to bring them in, they would have to notify the authorities in Aruba, and we were frightened that tipping them off would kill the meeting.

Deepak expressed concern about his brother's safety while traveling in the United States. But Larry assured him that a limousine would pick them up at the airport and take them directly to the meeting. Deepak seemed more concerned about meeting girls and having a good time than anything else. Larry promised him that the trip would be exciting.

Our goal was to have Deepak and Satish open up, and with enough money being waved in their faces, we hoped they would spill the beans. Larry put the thought in Deepak's mind that the bigger and better the story, the more money he could possibly receive. Deepak's greed was obvious. Soon, he became demanding, insisting on getting $500,000 up front. His attitude was that if we wanted the story, we would have to pay for it before he told us anything. After his exposure on the *Dr. Phil* show, he was apprehensive about letting us in on anything up front at all, especially if it was incriminating. But publishers do not deal that way. They need to know what they are laying out money for. So the situation turned into a catch-22, because Deepak would not open up without dollars on his plate.

I was then faced with a major dilemma. Do I pay the person who might have had something to do with the disappearance of my daughter without knowing whether or not he would offer up anything that we could use to find out what happened to her? We have a $1,000,000 reward for finding Natalee and a $250,000 reward for clues. I cannot give it to someone who does not deserve it on the off chance that he tells us what we want to know. But, in my heart, I believed that a resolution warranted doing anything just to have closure.

Deepak sent an e-mail that was extremely demanding and controlling. We decided to play hardball in the hopes that he would give in and offer us some information. So Larry cut off contact with him. The holidays passed, and we received no word from him. Then, on January 9, 2006, Larry spoke with him. Deepak told him that he had held off on doing anything, because he was told that if he came to the United States, he could not go back to Aruba for five years due to visa issues, but that he was still working with his attorney on coming here. Larry then suggested that Satish come here on his own if all else fails. If he were not willing to send Satish, then the worst case scenario would be building a level of trust with Deepak to ensure that the information he offers could be represented to the publisher through Larry. The mere possibility that we could get the boys to admit any criminal acts against Natalee was enough to keep trying to get him to come here where American officials could arrest him. If we could do that, maybe they would tell all. Larry left it to Deepak to decide if he was going to come to the United States or just convey information from home thinking he would get a huge book deal. Regardless of what he chose, it was incredible that Larry was actually conversing with the Kalpoe brothers. Knowing that time was running out on Deepak finding out about this book and that Larry has been working with me, we needed to get as much information as fast as possible. I was hoping that we would finally be able to get to the bottom of the heartbreaking mystery surrounding Natalee's disappearance and put it to rest once and for all. As of this writing, we are in the process of bringing in a major news organization to collaborate with us to expose possible inconsistencies with Deepak's stories.

On February 16, 2006, Joran van der Sloot and his parents, Anita and Paulus, arrived in New York City to be interviewed by ABC's *Primetime*. Upon their arrival, Joran and Paulus were personally served with a lawsuit filed by me and Beth. According to reports, Paulus was served at his hotel while Joran, after catching a plane from Holland and transferring in London to continue on to the United States, sat unaware that a former Scotland Yard investigator had boarded the connecting flight and was sitting three rows ahead of him. The moment the plane touched down on American soil, the investigator turned and served Joran.

The lawsuit alleges three causes of action against Joran, including injury to a minor child, false imprisonment, and intentional and malicious interference with custodial relations. Paulus is accused of negligent supervision of Joran in that he "knowingly facilitated his own son's predatory and tortuous behavior toward Natalee Holloway."

It is now America's turn to try to uncover the truth.

Support for our cause has grown enormously. There is no question that awareness of the way that Aruban officials have mishandled her case has become extremely widespread. Most often, we receive encouragement in our efforts to keep her story alive. However, there are times when the messages posted on the Internet give me the impression that people want us to drop this case. Sometimes they say that other missing persons should get as much, if not more, attention as Natalee.

Any publicity that Natalee's case receives does keep her story alive. But, more importantly, it keeps the issue of missing women in the forefront of the news. This is not just about Natalee anymore. Thousands of people go missing every year, and we need to do something to stop that from happening. By allowing us to keep Natalee in the news, to continuously verbalize our feelings about the people and the government that we feel are responsible for not getting to the truth about what happened to her, by demanding answers and insisting on new investigative teams in her case, we are letting the world know that we are not going to stand for one more person disappearing without a trace. We will not go away until we know what happened to our daughter and we are making a pledge that we will not stand by and allow this to happen to anyone else. We have just formed the "Natalee Holloway Foundation" to aid in the search for other missing persons, and I am in the process of developing a bill that I hope will be introduced into Congress, which will serve to protect American citizens traveling in foreign countries. As Americans, we live in a wonderful society that affords us the ability to take some things for granted, such as the assurance that criminal acts, especially those committed against our children, will be taken seriously from the moment of their inception. Had we been knowledgeable about the severe limitations of foreign investigations, we would have prevented our daughter from making the trip to Aruba. Unfortunately, we learned too late. But, we did the next best thing. We let the Aruban and Dutch authorities know that we are going to keep Natalee's story alive until we find out what happened to her.

We hope that everyone realizes that we have not received any special attention from the media. We have fought with all of our might for every bit of news coverage that we have gotten. We have never let up. We feel that we have had to fight to stay in the forefront so that nobody ever forgets what has happened to a wonderful young girl, our beautiful daughter, in a foreign country, because it could have happened to anybody's child. Is it selfish of us to continue with our campaign to remain as visible as we have? I am a father who gets into bed every night wondering what has happened to my daughter. The hours pass by very slowly, and my mind keeps going over all of the details in her case one by one. I try to drift off, only to think about one more possibility, one last thing that I might have missed. Did I ignore an e-mail that seemed too far-fetched only to miss the one real lead that would have solved the case of Natalee's disappearance? Did I stop digging one minute too soon at the landfill? Did I walk away from the Buddhist just before he was going to offer me Natalee for the reward money? What about the psychics? The theories? The rumors? The hypotheses? The opinions? Eventually, I have to stop torturing myself and go to sleep. I have to continue to investigate what happened to Natalee, and I also must keep up with my responsibilities as a husband and as a father to my three other children. So, I try to shut things out of my mind when I can and allow myself to drift off to sleep. It often seems like only five minutes have passed until the alarm goes off. I awaken hoping that it was all just a bad dream and that Natalee will come running in to talk to me. But when I open my eyes and call out her name, she doesn't answer. That's when I once again remember that my daughter is missing without a trace, and it is a very harsh reality.

I still have a strong feeling that Natalee is alive. I am not ready to face the other possibility. It may just be a father's wish, but a lot of people agree with me. I am confident that if we all work together, we will find an answer to what happened to my daughter.

We won't give up on you, Natalee. You didn't give up on us, and we will continue with the investigation until we have all of the answers to your disappearance.

God be with you, my Natalee!

Author's Note

I WROTE THIS BOOK WITH THE HOPE THAT IT WILL SERVE three important purposes: first, that someone somewhere will be encouraged to come forward with more information about Natalee's disappearance; second, to ensure that what happened to Natalee never happens to anyone else's child; and finally, that the "Natalee Holloway Foundation," funded by proceeds from this book, will aid others in their search for missing loved ones. If the information that I have divulged in this book saves just one individual from what Natalee went through, then I will rest easier knowing that my daughter's ordeal was not in vain.

With the help and support of so many wonderful people, Natalee has become the symbol for "Everybody's Child." You have allowed her into your homes as well as your hearts, and I, along with my family, truly thank you for caring so much.

Natalee, I love you. Fly high, my Freebird!

Appendix

SHANGO'S RIDDLE

As mentioned in chapter seven, I have attempted to do my own interpretation of Shango's Riddle with help from what I have read online and in e-mails. I've italicized the lines of the actual riddle and in parentheses offer possible interpretation. Before the riddle is a key to what the words in the code might mean. As I also said in chapter seven, all of what follows is open to interpretation, and nothing is meant to point fingers or lay blame at any one person or group of people. It is all suggestion and hypothesis, trying to make sense of a cryptic but possibly elucidating riddle.

KEY

These were the various participants and places referenced in the riddles:

Arawaks = These are the native Arubans.

Arawak King = This could be the prime minister of Aruba or possibly a boat of the same name that frequently travels to Aruba.

Babylon = The Dutch as a Protectorate of Aruba or Holland, or some see this as the Aruban police.

Babylonians = The Dutch population on Aruba. In ancient times, the Babylonians adopted and refined the ideas of the Sumarians.

Cowboy Gods = American higher ups, e.g. FBI.

Dicemen = Casino dealers on Aruba. Could refer to a boat that frequents Aruba called *Pair A Dice*. The reference to Dicemen might also be taken from an elite group of Marvel Comic Book characters where the Dicemen consist of rich, bored individuals looking for excitement. They set up situations through manipulation and trickery that create conflict among others. Then they sit back and enjoy the conflict while betting on the outcome.

Dice Throwers = Gamblers in the casinos.

DirtyHand = This character runs throughout the riddle. He is obviously a higher up in the chain of command on the island and a key player. Some refer to him as Jan van der Stratten, the chief of police. Others disagree.

Eden = Truth or innocence—it is where we all wish to be.

The Elders = The Dutch and Aruban authorities, and/or the parents of the boys.

Fallen Elder = Paulus van der Sloot, father of suspect Joran van der Sloot, was the most likely choice.

The Fly = Someone who entered the trap = Natalee.

Gods = Higher ups on Aruba and off island, possibly in the Dutch Province. Could be politicians, casino owners, police chief, etc.

The House of Rave = The party house where the music plays, some refer to this as Lorenzo's house.

The Lamb = Joran van der Sloot, main suspect, one of the last three people to be seen with Natalee, possibly he is being sacrificed to protect someone else.

The Lions = Those in the higher clique, at top level of illegal activity on Aruba, those considered to be untouchable, i.e. can get away with murder, possibly Natalee's murderers or kidnappers. There is a motel on the island near the VIP Club that is called the "Lion's Den." It is a very secluded place with guards. People have been seen entering with young girls and photography equipment.

Mary = Natalee.

The Maze = Houses where Raves are said to occur, e.g. The House of Rave.

Messengers = The Media, possibly Jossy Mansur.

The Music = Could refer to bad things that happened, or something that draws unsuspecting people in.

Roll = This may refer to taking "E" or Ecstasy; taking "E" is called "rolling."

Shivas = Brothers Deepak and Satish Kalpoe, two other main suspects.

Sumarians = Appeared at the beginning of time. Ideas were adopted and refined by the Babylonians, possibly *Diario* owner, Jossy Mansur, or government officials.

Threadsurfers = Bloggers.

Wampum = The Arubans' livelihood, their economy.

SHANGO'S RIDDLE

One straight path to the house of Rave, while of gold bricks the road is not paved. (The house of music where they hold parties is not the house of the wealthy. Leads one to believe it is not Lorenzo's house.)

Answers mysterious lie within. (The answers can be found in there.)

Magical letters which spell sin XTC DNA. (There is much speculation that XTC refers to different things. Someone has suggested that Joran has a half-brother named Lorenzo who had been in Aruba when Natalee was there, but went back to Holland for a while. Those who know Lorenzo say that his nickname is Xtacy, thereby referring to the XTC in the DNA. Others suggest that Natalee was given the drug Ecstasy.)

Babalu opened a window looking into Babylon. (Apparently, a blogger named Babalu solved one of the clues meant to lead people to seek the answer in the Dutch social structure or the Aruban police department.)

DirtyHand is alive. (Van der Stratten or another Dutch higher up is revealed.)

Shango said the key to the Hague did not exist. (The answer is not in any of the evidence sent to Holland.)

That door to Eden remains closed. (The truth is still hidden.)

Until the house with the path, But not of gold is entered. (Until the house where the raves are is found.)

DirtyHand walks with the Babylons, the Arawaks and is consort to the fallen elder. (Van der Stratten or another higher up is in with the Dutch or the Aruban police and also the native Arubans, and is deeply involved with Paulus van der Sloot.)

Outsiders brought into the Arawak tribe walk in many circles, nameless. (People who come to Aruba can mingle, but are unimportant.)

DirtyHand can bring down all houses. (Van der Stratten or another Dutch higher up can take down everyone.)

His reach is long. (He holds a lot of power over many people.)

Consort to all, except for the Gods. (Van der Stratten is involved with everyone except the Aruban higher ups.)

He knows the sacrifice is not responsible. (Van der Stratten knows Joran is not responsible for Natalee's disappearance.)

Of whom is the young Babylonian afraid? (Who is Joran afraid of?)

Why won't he talk? (Why doesn't he reveal the truth?)

The dice throwers know. (The casino dealers or boat owners know why Joran won't talk and why van der Stratten won't say Joran is innocent.)

The maze of the rave. (The way into the rave, house of music where parties are held, may not have a way out.)

And the fly that entered the trap. (Natalee Holloway was the fly.)

DirtyHand is the key. (Van der Stratten knows all.)

He walks in many circles. (He has contacts everywhere.)

Young Babylonians and Shivas do not build sand castles, did not play on the beach. (Joran and the Kalpoe brothers did not bring Natalee to the beach.)

DRAX SCORES. (Shango says that the blogger DRAX has uncovered the fact that the boys did not take Natalee to the beach.)

DirtyHand knows this. (Van der Stratten or other Dutch higher up knows that Natalee was not taken to the beach.)

Children of the Elders play in the maze. (The Aruban and Dutch kids party in the house of the Raves.)

But DirtyHand is afraid to rave. (Van der Stratten or other Dutch higher up does not go to the houses where the raves are held.)

Babylonians and Shivas do not play with sandcastles. (Look elsewhere because the answer is not at the beach.)

Follow the music! (Go to the house of the raves!)

Mary who was not a Virgin entered the maze to discover its secrets. (Natalee knew where she was going but did not know the dangers.)

The lamb is scared. (Joran is afraid.)

The fires are lit. (People are getting close to the truth.)

But now the lamb is a goat. (Joran is being made the scapegoat.)

Mary never heard the buoy toll. (Natalee did not realize she was in danger.)

Ask the men who play dice and "roll." (The casino dealers and those who gamble or do Ecstasy knew that Natalee was unaware of what was happening.)

Follow the music. (Stressing again to go to the house of raves.)

The DiceMen must be questioned. (The casino dealers must be questioned.)

They too go to the Music and enter the same Maze. (They go to the same parties.)

Mary who was not a virgin entered. (Natalee arrived.)

The DiceMen ROLLED. (They took Ecstasy.)

Mary ROLLED. (Natalee was slipped Ecstasy or knew she was taking it.)

Mary ROLLED through the Maze. (Natalee was on Ecstasy at the party.)

There is more than one house of music. (The right house must be found.)

The Lamb is a Scapegoat. (Joran is taking the fall.)

The Lamb returned to the fold. (Joran went back to Holland.)

Mary Rolled (Natalee was on Ecstasy.)

And the Lions played. (The untouchables did what they wanted to Natalee.)

Windows looking into Babylon are being opened by the ThreadSurfers. (The bloggers are figuring out what the Dutch or the Aruban police are doing.)

The maze offers many hidden desires. (The rave house has many secrets.)

Deflowerings of forbidden fruits. (They have a way of making girls give in to them.)

DirtyHand knows. (Van der Stratten or other Dutch higher up knows about it all.)

So does the elder. (So does Paulus van der Sloot.)

DirtyHand has walked through the maze. He knows of the forbidden fruit and the gardeners. (Van der Stratten or other Dutch higher up knows all about what is happening in the house of rave and the gardeners are those who get the girl and prepare her for the maze.)

Why do they leave the Maze open? (Why does the activity continue when van der Stratten or the Dutch higher ups are aware of it?)

Why hasn't an Arawak probed its fetid depths. (Why haven't the Arubans looked into what is obviously happening?)

It's not hidden and continues to operate. (It is happening right under everyone's noses.)

Tell the Cowboys! (Someone should tell the Americans!)

All know of the music, beckoning lost souls. (Everyone knows about the rave houses and what goes on in them.)

To enter the seven levels of inferno. (The number seven is significant— could be seven houses, seven rooms with various types of torture, seven levels of higher ups involved, seven levels of Dante's Hell.)

Who gave Mary the poison wine of Bacchus? (Bacchus was the God of wine. There was a cult in Rome dedicated to him and they held wild late-night orgies leaving everyone with terrible hangovers. The question asks who gave Natalee the drug? Was it the dealers, the bartenders at Carlos'n Charlie's, or someone she was with at the party?)

Enter the Maze. (Shango wants us to envision the maze.)

Babalu opened a window looking onto Babylon. (A blogger is correctly translating some of Shango's riddles.)

Some windows overlooking Babylon have been opened. (This refers to the bloggers who are understanding the riddle.)

But they can't hear the music. (But they don't have the answer yet.)

Stupid Cowboys with Arawak Guides. (It's like the blind leading the blind, having the Arubans help the Americans.)

Cowboys don't read smoke signals. (The signs are there, but the Americans aren't reading them correctly or they are ignoring them.)

They must enter the maze! (They must find the house of raves!)

Shango needs to feed the messengers. (Shango gives out information when pressured to do so. Could indicate Jossy Mansur is Shango.)

The Gods are talking. (All of the Aruban and Dutch higher ups are talking.)

Mary rolled into the maze. (Natalee was drugged before she went to the party.)

To play with Lions. (She went there thinking she would have a good time.)

But it was not a game. (She had no idea of the danger.)

The lamb ran bleating, afraid to walk through the maze. (Joran got scared and either left her or was thrown out, but he would never tell.)

Why don't the Arawaks ambush the Lions? (Why do the Arubans allow this to continue?)

The cowboys don't know. (The Americans have not caught on.)

DirtyHand knows, but is afraid of the Arawak Nation. (Van der Stratten knows all, but he will not stop it because of the scandal it will cause. The economy will suffer greatly and everyone will turn on him.)

The Simian was incorrect about the package from the Hague. (The Simian is apparently a blogger. It is possible that Simian and Shango are Deepak and Satish Kalpoe. Shango is saying that Simian guessed something about the evidence sent to Holland, but his guess was wrong.)

I told the Simian, but the Simian would not listen. (Simian had it right in front of him, but ignored it.)

The Simian is not a Simian, but an Australopithecus. (Shango is calling Simian one of the most primitive humans, e.g. a gorilla or a chimp. Australopithecus is interpreted as being the lowest form of brain capacity man may have ever evolved from.)

Threadsurfers on other beaches are oblivious to the Maze and the Lions. (Only the Arubans know what goes on in Aruba.)

Without exposure, the Arawaks will deceive the cowboys. (If someone doesn't come forward with the truth, nobody will find it.)

They will leave without loot. (Natalee will not be found.)

Shango is the god of justice. (Shango feels like the riddle will make justice prevail. The truth is that if Shango knows the truth, he is as bad as the rest of the criminals for playing a game with it.)

Alive in many forms he who speaks through Oxum through lightning and himself through thunder father of the violent dance diviner of secrets of the seven levels of inferno bound to truth even as it burns, so that justice may be brought. (Shango will reveal the truth even though he will be in danger.)

Only those who cRave music go into the Maze . . . (Only those who crave drugs and want to party will go into the house of rave.)

The Gods of Babylon have orchestrated the refrain for the Arawak choir. (The Dutch or Aruban police have created their story and the native Arubans speak it.)

The music which holds the answers lies within the maze. (The answers lie in the house of rave.)

The cowboys will smile sweetly as the chorus sings. (Since the Arubans continue to stick to their story, the Americans will believe them.)

Backs turned to the maze. (The Arubans do not approve of the house.)

From the poison song. (So they continue to tell the story.)

All the Arawaks know the Maze which plays the poison songs. (Yet, the Arubans know what goes on in the raves.)

How those innocent young flies enter the trap with honey laden notes. (How the virgin or unsuspecting girls are lured in and believe the lies.)

Shango must leave to feed the messengers. (Shango must talk to the media.)

Shango the God is sad because he sees history repeating itself, a new set of Lions is being created. (Shango has seen this all before and the higher ups or the untouchables are all being replaced, but the crimes are still the same.)

The Gods are talking. (All of the Aruban and Dutch higher ups are talking.)

Follow the notes. (Listen for the music.)

To the poison house. (The house where the drug was given to Natalee, where bad things happen.)

Where the children of the Babylonians and the Arawak nation meet, the school under cover of delusion. (The Dutch and Aruban children think they are equals, they meet at the house of rave with the victims)

In the maze. (When they play in the house of rave.)

The Lions which play shall be found. (The untouchables can be identified.)

The gamblers also took note. (The gamblers are betting on who will win.)

Tell the cowboys! (An exclamation point to emphasize the importance of making the Americans aware.)

Not all Lions leave their den. (Someone always stays at the rave house, a clue to help identify it.)

That which is hidden shan't be found in the light. (Natalee is in a dark place, or is only revealed at night.)

Babylon is Falling. (People are becoming aware.)

The Arawak teepees will be crushed. (The Aruban economy will suffer.)

Will they sacrifice the Lamb or the Lion? (Will Joran take the fall or will the truth be told?)

To make the cowboys smile. (Will the Americans accept Joran as the criminal or will the Arubans tell the truth?)

The Arawaks must hunt the Lions. (The Arubans must end this.)

In the place of darkness. (Where Natalee is.)

House of secrets. (The house where Natalee went.)

The Babylonian and the shivas did not build castles in the sand. (Joran and the Kalpoe brothers did not take Natalee to the beach.)

They lost to the Lions. (The untouchables took over with Natalee and told Joran to leave.)

DirtyHand knows the elder knows and so do the Arawaks. (Many people are aware of the truth.)

The cowboys are far from the house of Babylon. (The Americans are on the wrong trail.)

The maze shall remain dark. (No one will uncover the truth and the house will keep its secrets and continue.)

To all but the Arawak nation and the elders. (And the Arubans and higher ups will continue to allow it to happen.)

Shango has not danced with the Lions, nor Arawaks, and does not keep their company. (Shango is not one of the bad people or the Arubans; wants us to know he or she is good; Shango has not entered the guarded motel or the rave houses.)

Eyes of God may look from afar with great acuity. (The higher ups know more than we think. Could mean the investigators have more information to go on.)

The resolution to find Mary lies with the Arawak Nation. (The Arubans have the answer to what happened to Natalee.)

DirtyHand has bound the Arawak Nation with Babylonian Rope. (A higher up, possibly Van der Stratten, has tied the Arubans' hands due to Dutch control or through the Aruban police force.)

The Lamb and the two Shivas whisper in the dark. (Joran and the Kalpoe brothers know the secrets.)

While the Lions pace silently in the bush. (While the bad people wait quietly; the motel is out in the middle of nowhere and alarms sound when anyone comes close.)

DirtyHand is the link! (The higher up, possibly van der Stratten, holds the key.)

The lamb, the Shivas, the elder whispering, exiting like thieves in the night, clothed with invisible armor. (Joran, the Kalpoe brothers, Paulus van der Sloot, all got away with what they did.)

If DirtyHand falls, so does Babylon, but too, the Arawak Nation shall suffer. (If the higher up, van der Stratten, is taken down, the Dutch or the Aruban police force will also fall, but Aruba itself will also suffer, i.e. economy.)

Threadsurfers listen! (Bloggers, hear what I say.)

The lamb shall run anew in virgin fields, cropping sweet grass which should remain untouched. (Joran will find new victims at school in Holland.)

The Lamb has sins, but the Lions have sharper teeth. (Joran has done bad things, but the untouchables or motel owners are worse.)

A new key must be found to open unknown doors. (There is a piece of evidence that nobody has yet.)

The first concern of the Arawak nation is wampum. (The Arubans are worried about losing their livelihood.)

But unseen tides pull Babylonian seas through Arawak Moats, bittering the waters. (The Dutch on Aruba are intruding in what goes on behind the scenes in Aruba, making problems for the Arubans.)

DirtyHand and the Lions must see the light of Arawak Day, or forever walk in plentiful fields. (The higher up, possibly van der Stratten, and the untouchables must become aware that native Arubans will one day rise up against them.)

The dead shall eternally sleep if a clamour is not made. (The truth will not be revealed without pressure on those responsible.)

Lamb and the Elder are stepping stones into the fetid pool of deception. (Joran and his father, Paulus van der Sloot, know the answers.)

The rule of the Arawak King is the Final word. (The Prime Minister rules. Could also be that the boat holds the key.)

DirtyHand has fouled the air for all nearby, but the Arawak Nation will claim Babylonian. (The Dutch higher up, or van der Stratten, has made trouble for all involved, and the native Arubans have the ability to uncover what the Dutch do on Aruba.)

Authority prevents them from hunting Lions, and DirtyHand. (The untouchables and the higher ups are too well connected to be found out.)

But the Arawak King controls destiny of all. The Arawak King has DirtyHands and DirtyFeet. If he is to reign anew, he cannot be soiled more. (Could be that the Prime Minister or other higher up must keep his image intact or he won't be reelected.)

The Babylonians have ruled the Arawak Nation through deception and stealth, and their charges, the Arawaks, speak now with the same forked tongue, on behalf of their king. (The Dutch rule the Arubans through corruption, and the Arubans go along with them to protect the higher up, possibly the prime minister.)

The gift the cowboys ask of the king of the Arawak Nation is a mere trifle. (What the Americans ask of the prime minister is not important to him.)

All ye who sing in the cyber-chorus lower your voices not! (Bloggers must continue to push for an answer.)

It has been proven that the lamb, the shivas, and the elders are not the breach in Arawak Armour! (Joran, the Kalpoe brothers, and the Dutch parents or officials have not been able to gain the Aruban's complete loyalty.)

Let us hunt Lions, The King, and DirtyHand. (We should go after the untouchables, the prime minister or other Aruban higher ups, and van der Stratten or other Dutch higher up.)

The Lions pace silently in the bush, while the king seeks pleasures with his concubines. (The untouchables await their next prey while the higher up enjoys his position of control.)

Threadsurfers! What is sought is not hidden. (Bloggers, the answer is out in the open.)

The Lamb and the elder are not the keystone in the Arch of Corruption. (Joran and his father are not on the top rung of the conspiracy.)

Seek ye DirtyHand and the Fetid Arawak King who wishes to blame the Babylonians for the behaviour of lowly minions. (Look to the Dutch official and the prime minister rather than to the boy and his father to find the real criminals.)

If the head of the beast is in plain view it is folly to attack protected flanks. (The true criminal is out in the open while we are going after those who are protected.)

Threadsurfers, DirtyHand is more vulnerable than the Arawak King and your lances should point in his direction. (Bloggers, van der Stratten, or another Dutch higher up will fall faster than the Prime Minister, and bloggers should turn their accusations to him.)

He is the weak link, if he tumbles, all fall with him, the lamb, the shivas, the elder. (Van der Stratten or other Dutch official is the one to take down, because the rest will fall, too, Joran, the Kalpoe brothers, and Paulus van der Sloot.)

Shango looks from afar but speaks with truth. He does not converse with the Simian, or any other worldly sources, and attempts to bring direction to speculation. (Shango, the one who posts the messages stands on the outside looking in, but knows the truth. He is not involved with another blogger, Simian, or any other people who may know the truth. He is trying to show who is on the right track about what happened to Natalee.)

I must feed the messengers. (Shango talks to the media.)

The Gods are talking. (The higher ups, the Americans, the Dutch, the Arubans, are all communicating with each other.)

Index